"Joanna Harader's liturgies and prayers have formed my worship life for over a decade. I am delighted that her soothing, bold, and prophetic Advent reflections will be with me through the season of waiting. In prayers like poems and meditations that weave together the stories of women in the Bible with the lives of readers, Harader offers a gentle invitation: sit, wait, hold on, and don't give up."

MELISSA FLORER-BIXLER, author of *How to Have an Enemy* and lead pastor of Raleigh Mennonite Church

"With an ear for the word of Scripture, an eye for connections, and a pen that sings, Rev. Harader has brought the stories of eight women into our Advent and Christmas season as a gift. She offers reflective prisms to see the unique hues of each woman's story, and in those stories, she reveals the sometimes messiness of our humanity and what it means to have 'God with us' in the midst of the messiness."

DR. DAVID M. MAY, Landreneau Guillory Chair of Biblical Studies at Central Seminary

"If you long to drink from a well of unexpected richness and depth in this season of our Savior's birth, *Expecting Emmanuel* is the devotional you've been waiting for. Alongside beautiful artwork from Michelle Burkholder, these readings and blessings provide a fresh lens through which to consider the embodied experiences of the women who anticipated the arrival of Jesus. Accept this invitation to journey into the complex, sometimes messy stories you think you know and discover anew the life-changing power of 'God with us.'"

STEPHEN MATTSON, author of *On Love and Mercy: A Social Justice Devotional*

T0001473

"Lyrically written with pastoral sensitivity, *Expecting Emmanuel* offers a fresh reading of key texts featuring the women related to the story of Jesus. From ancient forebears and proximate characters, we learn again the theological richness of women's participation in the redemptive work of God. Joanna Harader's writing is theopoetics at its best—crafting images and insights that stir the heart."

REV. DR. MOLLY T. MARSHALL, president of United Theological Seminary of the Twin Cities

"This book is a gift, filled with beautiful prose and powerful testimony, both of which are fitting in telling women's stories. For far too long, the women in the story of Jesus' birth have been ignored, other than a brief and often reluctant nod in Mary's direction. Not only would this book make a good present to give at Christmas, but it is a gift to the church."

REV. DR. MIKE GRAVES, Wm. K. McElvaney Professor of Preaching and Worship emeritus at Saint Paul School of Theology and scholar in residence at Country Club Christian Church in Kansas City

EXPECTING EMMANUEL

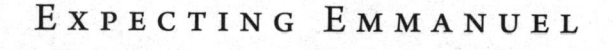

An Advent Devotional

EXPECTING

EIGHT WOMEN WHO PREPARED THE WAY

EMMANUEL

JOANNA HARADER

Original artwork by Michelle Burkholder

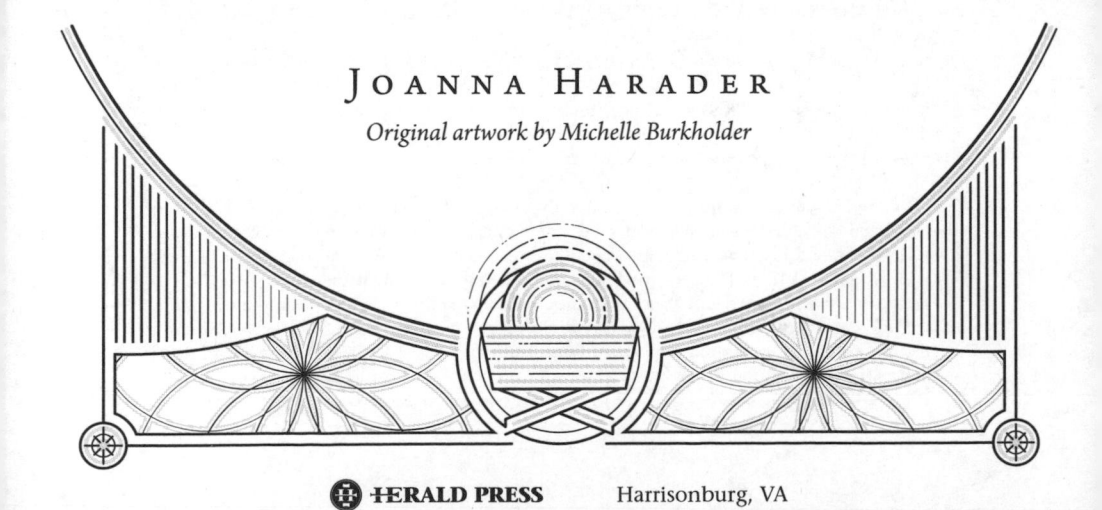

HERALD PRESS   Harrisonburg, VA

Herald Press
PO Box 866, Harrisonburg, Virginia 22803
www.HeraldPress.com

Library of Congress Cataloging-in-Publication Data
Names: Harader, Joanna, author. | Burkholder, Michelle, illustrator.
Title: Expecting Emmanuel : eight women who prepared the way / Joanna
   Harader ; original artwork by Michelle Burkholder.
Description: Harrisonburg, Virginia : Herald Press, [2022]
Identifiers: LCCN 2022015432 (print) | LCCN 2022015433 (ebook) | ISBN
   9781513810553 (paperback) | ISBN 9781513810560 (ebook)
Subjects: LCSH: Advent. | Christmas. | Jesus Christ. | Women in the Bible.
   | BISAC: RELIGION / Christian Living / Devotional | RELIGION / Christian
   Living / Spiritual Growth
Classification: LCC BV40 .H35245 2022 (print) | LCC BV40 (ebook) | DDC
   242/.33--dc23/eng/20220527
LC record available at https://lccn.loc.gov/2022015432
LC ebook record available at https://lccn.loc.gov/2022015433

Study guides are available for many Herald Press titles at www.HeraldPress.com.

EXPECTING EMMANUEL
© 2022 by Joanna Harader. Distributed by Herald Press, Harrisonburg, Virginia 22803.
   800-245-7894. All rights reserved.
Library of Congress Control Number: 2022015432
International Standard Book Number: 978-1-5138-1055-3 (paperback); 978-1-5138-1056-0 (ebook)
Printed in United States of America
Original artwork on pages 30, 46, 68, 88, 107, 125, 132, 138, and 143 by Michelle Burkholder

Unless otherwise noted, scripture text is quoted, with permission, from the *New Revised Standard Version*, copyright © 1989, Division of Christian Education of the National Council of Churches of Christ in the United States of America. Scripture quotations marked (AMP) are taken from the *Amplified® Bible*, Copyright © 2015 by The Lockman Foundation. Used by permission. www.lockman.org. Scripture quotations marked (ASV) are taken from the *American Standard Version*. Scripture quotations marked (ESV) are taken from the *ESV® Bible* (*The Holy Bible, English Standard Version®*), Copyright © 2001 by Crossway, a publishing ministry of Good News Publishers. Used by permission. All rights reserved. Scripture quotations marked (MEV) are taken from the *Modern English Version*. Copyright © 2014 by Military Bible Association. Used by permission. All rights reserved.

26 25 24 23 22   10 9 8 7 6 5 4 3 2 1

To the women of my genealogy, especially my grandmother Ruth, who is as bold and delightful as her biblical namesake; and my mother Cheryl, who has nurtured my deep love of Scripture

CONTENTS

INVITATION

Do you love Christmas music and lights and cookies but also long for more substance and depth to the season? Do you hate Christmas music and lights (does anybody hate cookies?) and also long for more substance and depth to the season?

Do you like the *idea* of using a devotional, but feel uninspired by most of the actual devotionals you see?

Do you look at the lovely nativity scenes that emerge at this time of year and roll your eyes because you know that there's a lot of blood and sweat and noise unaccounted for there?

Are you fascinated by the beautiful messiness of humanity and utterly astounded that God, our divine Creator, would actually *become human* for us?

If you answered yes to any of these questions, then welcome to this Advent and Christmas journey.

Over the weeks of Advent, we will explore the lives of the five women who are listed in Jesus' genealogy, considering how their humanity connects with ours, how God is present with us all, and what it means to claim that the divine One became human in the infant Jesus. After Christmas, we'll meet a few other women connected to Jesus' early life. In the stories of these women, we encounter scheming, manipulation, and outright lies. We encounter seduction and sex. We encounter grief and abuse. We encounter a lot of complicated moral and spiritual questions that don't lend themselves to sweet, warm, Christmasy reflections. And in the midst of all this complexity, we encounter God.

To believe in the incarnation, that God became human in the person of Jesus, is to believe that humanity matters. It is to take our humanity—and the humanity of others—seriously, to hold it tenderly, to consider it honestly. If the Word truly became flesh, then attending to human emotions, human bodies, and human stories can help us understand the strangely present power of God in our all-too-human lives.

And so, over these next several weeks together, we will attend to the stories of these women who are listed in the genealogy of Jesus and who accompany Jesus in the earliest days of his life. I have sought to honor the Scriptures and these women by exploring their stories fully and honestly without glossing over the more troubling aspects of their lives. This means that some of the reflections deal with difficult topics, including sexualized violence. Please be aware of your own sensitivity to these issues and tend well to yourself as you go through these readings. As I journeyed with these women in writing this book, I found that their very human stories held sacred space for my own humanity, for my own story. I pray you will find that the women hold this same sacred space for you as well.

I invite you to journey through this book—and this season—prayerfully. I invite you to read the stories of these women with sacred attention and to receive their wisdom with gratitude. I invite you to release the expectations of a "perfect Christmas" and to instead seek the experience of a holy season.

SUGGESTIONS FOR USING THIS DEVOTIONAL

The daily devotions in this book are dated to be used in any year, beginning on November 27 (the earliest possible start date for Advent) and going through Epiphany, January 6. Of course, life being what it is, you can read the entries when you get to them.

Each daily offering is either a devotional reading or a blessing. The devotionals contain a scripture passage; a reflection on that passage; a suggested spiritual practice to help you connect with yourself, God, or others; and several questions to consider. You might want to address the suggested questions intentionally by journaling about them or discussing them with others, or they may just be questions you carry lightly with you throughout your day.

The "Connect" activities are designed to give you a wide range of spiritual practices to engage during this season. Some people (like me) who get bored easily and love variety might appreciate having a new suggestion each day. Others may feel overwhelmed by so many options. I encourage you to engage these activities in whatever ways feel life-giving and energizing for you. Rather than trying multiple practices, you may feel drawn to dwell more often with one of the suggested activities. Some practices that could work well as companions to any of the devotionals are drawing and coloring as you pray (p. 42), contemplating visual images (pp. 67 and 121), listening to music or singing (p. 100), using a labyrinth (p. 118), and breath prayers (p. 141).

In addition to the devotional readings, you will also find blessings from these biblical women. I am delighted that my dear friend and colleague Rev. Michelle Burkholder agreed to create images to accompany these blessings—images that are, themselves, blessings. I encourage you to mark and go back to any of the blessings that feel especially meaningful to you as we journey together through Advent, Christmas, and Epiphany.

While this book is primarily designed for personal use, I have provided some guidance for those who would like to use it in a group setting. The Guides for Group Use starting on page 145 provide resources for using this material in worship, small group/Sunday school, and retreat settings.

However you engage with *Expecting Emmanuel*, I pray it will draw you closer to God in this holy season.

A NOTE FROM THE ARTIST

As a longtime admirer of Joanna's writing, I was thrilled and honored when she invited me into a space of collaboration for *Expecting Emmanuel*. The invitation was to create original visual art in response to nine blessings written from the perspective of women in Jesus' lineage. The process was both challenging and rewarding.

For many years, my primary art medium has been paper cutouts. A paper cutout is an image created by removing sections of a single sheet of paper. Lines and shapes come forth from the gaps and segments remaining on the page. It is a practice in planning, patience, persistence, and wonder.

I cautioned Joanna that I am not one to often create portraits. Much of my work is abstract—lines and shapes in a relationship of composition. If she was seeking images of the women offering these blessings, I was likely not the artist to ask. Joanna graciously assured me that the invitation was not about illustrating, or even representing, the women. It was instead an invitation to visual reflection on the content of the blessings.

With curiosity, I dug into the content of Joanna's written words. Each blessing is lovingly crafted with intention and care, offering a rich array of visual imagery. My imagination was immediately engaged. I read and reread the blessings, sitting with them, noting words, shapes, and emotions that arose in each encounter.

My work attempts to create a space of reflection and conversation between word and image. In freeing myself to let the art take shape as a response to each blessing, both the words and images seemed to expand. It is my hope that those who encounter these words and art join in the invitation to reflect on each as individual creations while also exploring them in relationship with one another.

—*Michelle Burkholder*

WOMEN PREPARE THE WAY

READ:
Matthew 1:1–17

REFLECT:
Perhaps you—or people you know (and possibly try to avoid)—are a little obsessed with your family tree. I'm not overly invested in mine, but I can tell you that somewhere down the line I had ancestors named Shadrach, Meshach, and Abednego Harader. And also a Dorothy Gale (yes, from Kansas). In reading through a list of family names, there are moments when the anonymous syllables take on a bit of flesh and call forth questions: Who was this person? Why did their parents choose that name? How badly were they teased because of it?

Besides our curious wonderings, there are also deeper truths revealed in our genealogies. Where did "our people" come from? Where were they displaced to? Did they displace others? Where is the trauma—and the resilience—lurking in these lists of names? For all the answers we find in our family trees, there are even more questions. A compassionate and critical tending to these questions raised by our own family histories can be an important piece of our personal growth and our work toward justice.

Genealogies can be somewhat complicated in many families that, like mine, involve adoption. We don't know much about the *biological* ancestors of my two oldest children, and sometimes that feels like a loss. But it's significant that Jesus' genealogy lists *Joseph's* ancestors, not Mary's. This is the family tree that Jesus was adopted into. The Bible acknowledges and honors many forms of family.

Today's scripture passage is one we generally skim over. It's a text no scripture reader wants to see in the bulletin. Still, I find this list of Jesus' ancestors to be one of the most beautiful and compelling passages in Scripture. Here at the beginning of Matthew's gospel, the author insists that Jesus has parents, and grandparents, and great-grandparents, and great-great-grandparents. Before the awe-inspiring story of Jesus' miraculous healings and wise words, before the declarations that he is the Messiah, before the crucifixion and resurrection, we have the genealogy.

The story of Jesus' birth is grounded in human history. It is not just the story of one young woman's awkward pregnancy, but the story of generation after generation of people living in this world, muddling through relationships, trying to find their way to God. This genealogy is an insistence on the incarnation. It is a declaration that when the Word became flesh, it became flesh in just the same glorious and mundane way that we all become flesh.

This genealogy is also an invitation into the rich history that is merely hinted at as we skim through the generations from Abraham to Jesus, "who is called the Messiah." Every name is a story. Every one of Jesus' ancestors had their own lives, their own loves, their own struggles and accomplishments. Every generation faced trauma—maybe also caused trauma—and tried to figure out how to follow God in the midst of it all.

Some of the names listed, like Jechoniah, Salathiel, and Eliud, we encounter only in these brief verses. We know nothing of their stories beyond how they fit into Jesus' family line. Others, of course, are well-known biblical figures: Abraham, Isaac, and Jacob; David and Solomon. And then there are the women: Tamar, Rahab, Ruth, Bathsheba, and Mary.

It is odd for the author of Matthew to include any women in this genealogy at all; Luke's list includes only men. But with these few female names, Matthew's gospel gives us a great gift. The women he names have rich stories that can speak deeply to us in these days of Advent. As we spend time with these women in the coming weeks, we will see how their stories connect to the Jesus story and to our own stories.

CONNECT:
Contact a woman who is part of your family tree (mother, aunt, grandmother, niece, daughter, etc.) and ask her to share a story from her life.

CONSIDER:
How have your ancestors—even the ones who died long before you were born—helped form who you are today? How do you think Jesus' ancestors influenced him? Why might the author of Matthew begin his gospel with a genealogy?

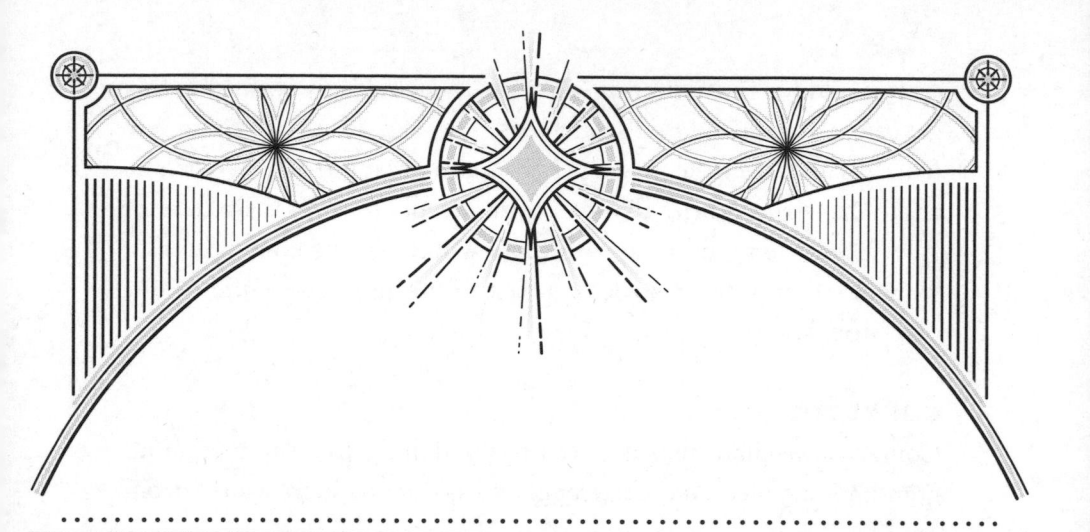

TAMAR

November 28

TAMAR GRIEVES

READ:
Genesis 38:1–11

REFLECT:
Tamar is the first woman listed in Jesus' genealogy, linked to the divine family lineage through marriage and deception. Yet before we really get to Tamar's story, we encounter the unnamed shadow figure of Judah's wife. No attention is given to the grieving mother, but she is there, in the background, joining ranks with Rachel and Mary, with my grandmother, my aunt, my friend. Tamar's mother-in-law is there bearing witness to the destabilizing grief of losing a child.

Judah's concern seems to be not with the loss of his son, but with the fact that he does not have an heir. Rather than words of lament from Judah, we hear words of problem-solving; he commands his second oldest son: "Go in to your brother's wife; . . . raise up off-spring for your brother" (Genesis 38:8). If Judah grieves his son's death, we know nothing of it.

We also know nothing of Tamar's grief. In this first part of her story, Tamar is treated as an object. Judah "takes" her as a wife for his oldest son, Er. And when Er dies, Judah tells his next oldest son, Onan, to "go in to" her, which he apparently does several times—and then he also dies. And after what must have been a fairly traumatic few years in Judah's household, Tamar is dismissed—told to go back to her father's house and wait for Er's youngest brother to come of age.

We don't know whether Tamar was taken as a wife against her will or whether she loved Er. The writer of this narrative says that Er was "wicked." Is that what Tamar thought? What were the consequences of his wickedness for her? Was he kind or abusive? Was she relieved or heartbroken—or a little of both—when he died? And what about Onan? Does she want her husband's brother to do this particular duty? Does she resent his refusal to impregnate her? Is she sad or angry or just confused by the whole mess? How does she feel when *he* also dies? And how does she feel about returning to her father's house? Is this a burden or a relief?

As we enter into "the holiday season," a kind of relentless cheerfulness is imposed on us from many sides: the jaunty music on the radio, the persistent holiday lights, the bright colors in the store displays. And I hope that you do find some happiness, even some joy, in the bright festivities of the season. But Advent is a time when we attend to the humanity of Jesus, which should allow us to attend to our own humanity as well. Our emotions, like Tamar's, may be quite complicated and messy.

The holiday season is often a time of increased tension within families, elevated stress as we try to fulfill too many roles, and deepening grief in the face of unrelenting cheer. The reality is that there is no right way to experience the relationships we have; no proper emotion to feel about any particular event or during any given time of year. Things that look terrible from the outside might actually bring positive feelings; things that seem wonderful to those looking in can make us feel awful. Grief is a shape-shifter that shows up in a thousand different ways. In this season of Advent, we can remember that through Jesus, God has experienced grief, and God is faithfully present with us in all our complicated emotions.

CONNECT:

Settle into a quiet and comfortable space. Hold on to a stone (or other solid object), take a deep breath, and name aloud who and what you are grieving in this season. Sit in silence for a few minutes, inviting the Holy Spirit to offer comfort and speak to your grief. Then place the stone in a place that will remind you of God's care and love (maybe outside in the sunshine or wrapped in a warm sweater in a drawer).

CONSIDER:

What emotions do you carry into this Advent season? What complicated grief do you bear? What joy do you hold? Do you have a sense that you *should* feel a particular way? What will help you accept your feelings as they are?

TAMAR WAITS

READ:
Genesis 38:12–23

REFLECT:
"In course of time." That brief phrase indicates Tamar's restless season of waiting. She is living in an in-between time: in her father's household, but belonging to Judah's household; a widow who is not free to marry; a woman obligated to have children with no legitimate way to conceive them.

"In course of time." We don't know how long it has been since Judah sent Tamar away, but we know it has been too long. Shelah, the youngest brother who is supposed to be her husband, has grown up, but Judah has not sent for her. She is still wearing her widow's garments, carrying her grief with no way to move forward. In a world where women are identified primarily by their relationships to men ("the wife of Judah, Shua's daughter"), Tamar's connection to men—and therefore her identity—is uncertain. She is a daughter still in her father's household, but not really. She is a wife married to nobody, but connected in marriage to three brothers. She is a should-be mother with no children.

Tamar has very little power in her situation. She is stuck—until someone tells her that Judah is going to Timnah to shear his sheep. I find myself wondering who that someone was. Did a family member assume that Tamar wanted to keep up on the family news and casually mention in passing where Judah was headed? Did Tamar have a friend, a co-conspirator who helped her keep track of Judah and plot her action? However Tamar receives this news, she uses her knowledge of Judah's travel as a means to get herself unstuck. She has waited around long enough. She has played the role she was supposed to play for a "course of time." Now she is ready to stop waiting for Judah to do the right thing and take action to make Judah do the right thing.

Everything about Tamar's actions here is deliberate and wise. She puts on appropriate clothing. She wraps herself in a veil so that Judah will not recognize her. She places herself at the entrance to one of the towns that Judah will be traveling through—a location that might, and in fact does, lead Judah to believe she is a prostitute. Did Tamar know that Judah was in the habit of "going in to" prostitutes? Did she imagine he would be sexually needy since his wife had died? Did she calculate that Enaim was far enough from his home that he would feel free to approach her? With the knowledge she has, Tamar sets the scene perfectly.

Once Judah makes his sexual interest known, Tamar asks what he will pay, and she negotiates this deal skillfully. She doesn't actually want the sheep that Judah promises; she wants the pledge—the signet and cord and staff. It seems a lot for him to give, but she presents it as a reasonable request, as nothing to be concerned about. And so he hands over these personal items to someone he believes to be a stranger. And he "goes in to" her. With this one act of intercourse, Tamar gains her ultimate goal: she becomes pregnant. Which makes me think that she likely thought through the timing of this encounter in terms of her own fertility cycle as well.

It is a masterful plan. A plan that indicates Tamar's deep understanding of human nature in general and Judah's nature in particular. In carrying out this plan, Tamar ends her own time of waiting; she gets herself unstuck.

We talk about waiting a lot during Advent. And there are certainly times to wait patiently for what is to come. We wait for babies to be born. We wait for seasons (literal and metaphorical) to change. We wait to learn and grow and be ready for new experiences. We wait on our God, who will renew our strength (Isaiah 40:31).

Waiting on God, on the natural cycles God has established, is good and holy. But waiting on other people, as Tamar has waited on Judah, is sometimes harmful. We can get stuck when we set aside our own autonomy and power to wait for another person to make things right for us. I admire Tamar for using the resources at her disposal to get herself unstuck, for deciding that the time had, in fact, run its course.

This Advent season of waiting does not mean a season of passivity. It does not mean a season of powerlessness. Our waiting on God renews our strength and can help us take the actions we need to get unstuck.

CONNECT:

Write the first part of Isaiah 40:31 ("Those who wait for the LORD shall renew their strength") on a piece of paper or card stock. Place the paper somewhere that you will see it each day and be reminded that you are called to wait for God *and* to use your strength.

CONSIDER:

What has been the hardest season of waiting in your life? What are you waiting for right now? *Whom* are you waiting for right now? Is your waiting part of a natural, healthy rhythm, or is it a time of being stuck? If you are stuck, what steps could you take to get unstuck?

TAMAR REFUSES SHAME

READ:
Genesis 38:24–30

REFLECT:
"Played the whore" (Genesis 38:24) is a phrase intended to shame Tamar; these words are used to condemn her for having sex outside of marriage. Judah, who has relegated Tamar to her unmarried yet obligated status, is more than ready to punish her for her perceived transgression: "Bring her out and let her be burned." What he doesn't realize is that Tamar has, quite literally, "played the whore"—in particular she has played the role of whore for *him*.

I wonder who brings Tamar out to be burned? Who is willing to murder someone because of a perceived sexual violation? Who is so loyal to Judah that they would set fire to a pregnant woman because he said so?

I wonder, also, how Tamar feels when she is brought out to be burned. She is confident she is in the right, and she has the evidence to prove it. Still, justice does not always prevail. People do not always admit their wrongs, no matter how glaring. There is a very real chance that Tamar will in fact be killed. But she keeps to her plan—she sends the signet, cord, and staff to Judah, and she waits.

In her waiting to be married to Shelah, Tamar decided to take matters into her own hands. As she waits to learn whether her death sentence has been commuted, there is nothing she can do. As readers, we learn of her fate in the very next verse, but we don't know how long Tamar waits. It says that she "sent word" to Judah (v. 25). This suggests that Tamar is bound and being prepared for burning while someone travels to take the items to Judah, while Judah responds, and then while someone travels back to Tamar's executioners with the news. That whole time she is waiting to learn whether she will live or die.

There are limits to our power. Not everything is within our control. Sometimes, waiting—and praying—is all we can do. Waiting and praying and sticking to the plan. Tamar surely knew the plan was risky when she undertook it. There were so many places where so many things could go wrong. And in the end, she had to depend on the honesty and honor of a man who had proven himself to be dishonest and dishonorable.

But when Judah sees the three items Tamar sends, he recognizes that the shame is his, not hers. The shame he feels is not about sleeping with a prostitute, but about refusing to allow Tamar to marry his youngest son; it is about relegating her to childlessness because of his own fears. The fact that Tamar has twins seems to justify her actions; she receives a double reward for her intelligence and bravery. Her refusal to passively accept Judah's mistreatment and her refusal of the shame he tried to impose on her lead to her great honor in bearing twin boys.

Just as Judah seeks to shame (and kill!) Tamar for her sexual "sins," so there are shaming forces all around us today. We might hear words from other people, see images, or read material that leads us to feel shame about some aspect of our lives: our bodies, our parenting (or childlessness), our relationships, our gender expression, our sexuality, our health, our job. Too often we are made to feel that there is one *right* way to be, one *right* way to act, even though we are all unique individuals experiencing a wide variety of circumstances.

It is a bold and brave thing to refuse the shame others would place on us. And it is a difficult and faithful thing to consider others as individuals and refuse to place shame on them for choices they make that we cannot possibly understand. Perhaps remembering Tamar's story can help us be brave and faithful, refusing to be shamed and refusing to place shame on others.

CONNECT:

Tie a piece of red thread (or yarn or ribbon) around your wrist to remind you of Tamar's twin sons—of the honor we can receive when we refuse shame and act with brave faith. Think of a word that feels empowering to you, and offer that word as a prayer throughout the day as you see and touch the thread.

CONSIDER:

What shame do you need to reject in your life? Have you taken necessary actions that others have labeled shameful? Is there something about your identity that others condemn? Or maybe you are more in the position of Judah, and should consider the assumptions you are making about others and the shame you may be—intentionally or unintentionally—putting on them.

TAMAR'S BLESSING

It is not your fault,
    but it is your grief—
    the deaths of those you have loved,
    the betrayals of those who should be trustworthy,
    the ways you have been neglected,
    and the shame they have invoked to kindle the fires.

It is your grief,
    but it is not your fault.

No matter what they say,
    you are free,
    in God:

Free to cry into the night, to wail and weep
    and to wear your widow garments for exactly as long as you like;
    free to name those who betray you—
    in private and in public—with truthful words, proper or not.

Free to insist on your own existence and importance,
    to take up whatever space your body and soul need to inhabit.

Free to turn the shame back on those who deserve it,
    to light the fires that warm and enlighten
    rather than those that destroy.

Wear this blessing as a signet,
    tie it around your waist as a cord,
    carry it as a staff, to support and protect:

May the God of cloud and fire
    lead you in the wilderness,
    providing room for your grief,
    support for your anger,
    comfort for your pain,
    attention to each part of you.

May the God of cloud and fire
    burn away your shame
    to reveal your shining wisdom,
    your unmistakable power.

RAHAB

December 2

RAHAB SHELTERS SPIES

READ:
Joshua 2:1–7

REFLECT:
"Two men" went into "the house of a prostitute whose name was Rahab," and someone told the "king of Jericho" about the visit.

That's odd, don't you think? That Israel's top spies are just "men," and the ruler of the entire nation is "the king," while the prostitute alone gets a name? This isn't usually how the biblical text works. Scripture is littered with unnamed women, but this particular woman, Rahab, is named—here in this narrative, in two of the New Testament epistles, and in the genealogy of Jesus.

Rahab is named, and her occupation is highlighted. While on the one hand her status as a prostitute diminishes, and possibly shames, her, it is also true that this status is the reason "the men" are able to talk with her at all. "Respectable" women would be in the home of their father or husband and would not be able to speak openly with unrelated men. As two strange men in a foreign town, where else could the spies go but a brothel? What other women could they approach?

Rahab lives—literally and figuratively—on the border. Her house is built into the wall of the city. Her occupation places her outside mainstream culture. Her willingness to help foreign spies suggests that she does not feel a deep connection or loyalty to the people in her community. Inhabiting this type of marginal space is often uncomfortable. It can be inconvenient to live on the outskirts of town. It can be difficult to function outside the realm of respectable society. It can feel lonely to be disconnected from your community.

Yet Rahab's place on the edge gives her many advantages. As we will see in tomorrow's reflection, the location of her home in the city wall proves quite convenient for a woman harboring spies. And while her occupation as a prostitute places her outside the boundaries of respectability, it also affords her a freedom not granted to other women in her culture—the freedom to have a house of her own and to talk freely to men outside her household. Furthermore, her disconnect from her community means she feels no obligation to obey the king's orders. Because of Rahab's marginal status, she risks less than most of her neighbors would in aiding the foreign spies. This entire story depends on Rahab's position on the literal and metaphorical edges of her community.

Those of us trying to follow Jesus in the world today likely find ourselves on the edge of a lot of things, not quite understanding many of the people around us, not really fitting into the dominant culture, not fully able to commit our loyalty to the rulers and powers who expect, even demand, it. Existing in the margins is often inconvenient, difficult, even lonely. But Rahab's story reminds us that there are also advantages to dwelling on the edge.

It is from the edge that we get a more complete and clear perspective of the situation. With her home embedded in the wall of the city, Rahab is positioned to see both those within and those outside her community. From the edge, we may have more opportunities to encounter people who are different from us—and who might have something valuable to offer. Ironically, Rahab's socially marginalized position allows her to speak with people—both the foreigners and the king's men—whom she would not have contact with if she were a "respectable" woman. Being on the edge means that we have little to lose and, therefore, will likely be willing to take more risks and confront those in power.

As we journey through Advent, it is worth noting that many of Jesus' ancestors existed on the edge in some significant way. And it is worth remembering that Jesus himself was far removed from the center of political and religious power. Sometimes being on the edge is the exact thing that puts us right in the middle of God's story.

CONNECT:

Find a physical space that is, somehow, on an edge. Maybe sit in a doorway or travel to a city or state line; maybe place yourself at the boundary of a piece of property or find a place where one terrain type transitions into another. Situate yourself in this marginal space; feel what it is to be on the edge of something. Talk to God about all the places in your life where you feel like you are on the margins. Ask God how you can be faithful in these marginal spaces.

CONSIDER:

Who is on the edge of a community or system in which you dwell closer to the center? Seek out their perspective by having a conversation, reading an article, listening to a podcast, or watching a video. What can you learn from them? Is God calling you to learn more, or maybe to take action on their behalf?

December 3

RAHAB NEGOTIATES A DEAL

READ:
Joshua 2:8–21

REFLECT:
I imagine Rahab finds the brightest crimson cord she can and ties it in her window as tightly as possible. After that, all she can do is pray that this flash of red will be enough to save her and her family from the soon-to-be-invading Israelites.

Like Tamar, Rahab does what she can to control her situation: she makes a plan, she negotiates to her advantage, she uses whatever leverage she can muster. And then she just has to wait. And she has to hope that the men who came to her—men who are untrustworthy by nature, because they are spies—will honor the commitment they made and spare the people in the house with the crimson cord.

I wonder whether the spies are surprised to find themselves at the mercy of this woman, this prostitute. At any point she could reveal their presence, which would likely lead to their death. To be sure, *if* the men get away safely and come back with an army to invade the city, Rahab will want to be on their good side. But if Rahab turns them in, they most likely won't survive to return with an invading force. It's questionable whether the Israelites could launch a successful attack without the intelligence that these two spies are set to provide.

Which leads to the troubling question of why Rahab would betray her own people to side with these foreigners. Does she have some grudge against the people of Jericho, perhaps for shaming her and pushing her to the edge of the city? Does she make a calculated assessment that the Israelites will be able to defeat her people and she just wants to side with the winners? Has she somehow developed a deep faith in the God of the Israelites and sees this as a way to serve God?

Read one way, this is a heroic story of a courageous and faithful woman. Rahab risks her own life to protect the lives of the Israelite men; she chooses to side with them because she believes in the power of their God. Read another way, this is a tragic story of how the calculating selfishness of Rahab leads to the genocide of her people.

As with most stories, the truth is probably somewhere in between these two extreme versions. Rahab was courageous, no doubt. And smart—and calculating. I'm sure she was also scared. And likely felt little connection or loyalty to the people in her community who had marginalized her throughout her life. Her community left her to fend for herself, and so that is exactly what she did.

I honestly don't know whether to frame Rahab as a hero or a villain; it depends on whose perspective you take. So perhaps it's best to just frame her as a brave, intelligent, complicated woman. A woman who was put into a difficult position and did the best that she could with what she had.

Many people face impossible choices every day: whether to pay for medicine or pay their rent; to do work that feels fulfilling or work that pays the bills; to pay off debt or pay for a bit of ease; to stay in the good graces of people they love or be honest and true to themselves. It is easy to judge people's choices from the outside, but perhaps Rahab can remind us that most people's lives are more complicated than we understand.

CONNECT:

Imagine an encounter between Jesus and Rahab. You might want to write a short script or just envision it in your head. How would they meet? What would they say? How would Jesus treat her, and how would she respond?

CONSIDER:

What can you do to make people feel included and not alienated in your communities? What can you do to ensure that the people in your community don't have to make so many difficult, unjust choices? How can you better understand people who make decisions with which you might disagree? How can you accept grace for yourself when you are faced with difficult choices?

December 4

RAHAB SURVIVES

READ:
Joshua 6:22–25

REFLECT:
After Rahab helps the spies escape, they go back to their camp and fill Joshua in on the situation. Then the Israelites launch their odd yet successful attack on the city of Jericho. The city walls fall, the valuables are looted, and everything else is burned.

Is this what Rahab had in mind when she hid the spies? As she observes the destruction around her, does she regret helping the Israelites, or is she glad to have chosen the winning side?

Amid all the morally problematic elements in this story, this concluding scene reveals a certain integrity on the part of Rahab and the Israelites—they all keep their promises. They stick to the agreement. After the spies left, Rahab could have gone to the king of Jericho and warned him about the impending attack. The Israelites certainly could have ignored the crimson cord and killed Rahab and her family along with everyone else. It's really somewhat surprising that they keep their word to someone society held in such low esteem.

I'm not sure Joshua is too happy about this agreement, actually. While the narrator uses Rahab's name, to Joshua she is "the prostitute" and "the woman." Still, he instructs the two spies to keep their promise—bring Rahab outside the city before the Israelites burn it. A small kindness in the midst of destruction.

That kindness extends not just to Rahab, but also to other members of her family. She insists that the spies promise to save "[her] father and mother, [her] brothers and sisters, and all who belong to them" (Joshua 2:13). And then, later, the spies bring out Rahab along with "her father, her mother, her brothers, and all who belonged to her" (6:23).

It is notable that neither of these lists include children or a husband. It seems that Rahab is unmarried and childless—which might be expected of a prostitute, but is definitely unusual in the scope of named women of the Bible.

In Tamar's story, her desire to be a mother propels the action of the narrative, and the birth of her twins provides the climax of the story. Likewise, the birth of Obed to Ruth serves as the satisfying conclusion to her story. The stories of Mary and Bathsheba center on their pregnancies and then on their roles as mothers. Of all the women in Jesus' genealogy, it is only Rahab who has a story in her own right with no mention of husband or child.

On the basis of Matthew's genealogy, we assume that Rahab eventually gave up her job as a prostitute and married an Israelite named Salmon (see Matthew 1:5), but we don't really know—because Rahab's marital status is not what is important to her story.

In white North American culture, the family unit of spouses and children is often prioritized over other forms of family; the role of parent (especially mother) takes on an all-important status. As we celebrate Advent and Christmas in the church, we talk a lot about pregnancy and motherhood and babies. We set up nativities of the holy family: Mary, Joseph, Jesus. But Rahab reminds us that families consist of far more than a partner and children. Our families include "[our] father and mother, [our] brothers and sisters, and all who belong to [us]" (Joshua 2:13). Sometimes our families consist of people who would not even show up in our genealogy.

Some people long to be spouses or parents, yet are not able to be for a variety of reasons. Other people choose not to marry or not to have children, again for a wide range of reasons. And for many people who do have children, their role as parent is not the defining narrative of their life. The connections we have to those we love—biologically related or not—are certainly important in our lives, but they are not our whole lives. Above and beyond our roles and relationships, we are, most importantly, children of God.

CONNECT:
Spend some time in prayer for the people with whom you have significant relationships. You might want to try praying with colored pencils, pens, or markers. Draw lines on a piece of paper (curvy or straight) to divide it into several sections and then write a name in each section, using colors and embellishments as you wish and praying for the people as you write and color. Carry this list of names with you or display it somewhere prominent as a reminder to give thanks for and pray for these people.

CONSIDER:
What roles do you have in relation to the other people in your life? Which roles feel like they are at the center of your story? Which roles do you feel most called to by God? Do any of these roles seem to keep you from living out God's call more fully? How could you find a balance between your relationship roles and your role as a child of God?

December 5

RAHAB ACTS BY FAITH

READ:
Hebrews 11:29–31; James 2:23–26

REFLECT:
Beyond the narrative in Joshua and Jesus' genealogy, Rahab is mentioned two other times in Scripture. Both times her name appears in a list of heroes of the faith, and it seems like a miracle that this woman, a prostitute with only a brief mention in the Hebrew Scriptures, manages to make the cut. The author of Hebrews lists several people who acted "by faith" and were thus rewarded. In this long and illustrious list, Rahab is the only woman commended for her faith. The author of James gives two examples of people "justified by works and not by faith alone" (2:24): Abraham and Rahab.

Clearly, Rahab loomed larger in the faith tradition than her brief story in the book of Joshua might suggest. She is, in a sense, the savior of those who would become her people; an exemplar of the type of faith in God that leads to courageous and significant works on behalf of God's people.

One might think that as her status in the community grew, her story might have been cleaned up a bit. We might expect the focus to shift from Rahab's earlier identity as a prostitute to her later identity as the wife of the Israelite Salmon and the mother of Boaz. Yet in both of these New Testament books, the authors identify this great hero of the faith as "Rahab the prostitute" (Hebrews 11:31; James 2:25).

I find myself wondering why the authors of both books would designate her in this way. Is this an attempt to diminish her even as they acknowledge her important role in Israelite history? "Sure, Rahab did some important stuff and we're listing her here with these guys, but don't forget she was a prostitute!" Or is the mention of Rahab's social position meant to emphasize the grace offered by God? "God can use anyone, even a prostitute!"

Why does Rahab alone have her morality questioned in the way she is identified? In the entire litany of the faithful from Hebrews 11, Rahab is the only one whose name is followed by any sort of qualifier. She is included with the men, but she cannot be just "Rahab" as the men are allowed to be identified solely by their names. She is "Rahab the prostitute," a label that defines her in relation to men.

Yet the full content of these two passages suggests that we all find our identity in our relationship with God, not in how other people view us. The authors of Hebrews and James may have viewed Rahab as a prostitute, but the crux of her identity was her faith in God and the courageous action she took.

When traditionally marginalized people are included in more mainstream contexts, there is often still a tendency to qualify their identities, to make sure that their marginal status is understood even as they may be placed alongside "important" figures. I am identified as a "woman pastor" far more often than my male colleagues are identified as "men pastors." Those with physical and mental differences often receive qualifiers with their identities: the blind writer, the athlete in the wheelchair, the autistic professor. People who identify with racial and ethnic minority groups know this experience well, as do LGBTQIA people.

Those who benefit from the status quo want to control how we are identified. And to a certain extent, we can't stop them: what they write gets into the history books; what they say gets broadcast over the airwaves. But in our own selves, in our own relationship with God, we can claim our pure identity as beloved children. In the context of God's reign, Rahab is not "Rahab the prostitute," or even Rahab the mother of Boaz; she is Rahab the faithful and courageous. May we also find our identity in our relationship to God.

CONNECT:

Sit in silence for at least three minutes and appreciate your identity as a child of God.

CONSIDER:

What labels have people given you? What labels have you given others? What labels have you given yourself? What is the difference between an identity and a label? To what extent is one's identity—be it gender, race, occupation, religion, relationship—important? In what ways does a focus on external identity diminish us? How can you claim your relationship with God as your central identity?

RAHAB'S BLESSING

Perhaps you have been there, too,
    on the edge,
    a mere windowsill away
    from being cast out completely.

Maybe you have been there, too,
    in the midst of uncertainty,
    having to choose the form
    of your own potential devastation.

It's possible you have been there, too,
    stuck with a label
    that is true and fine
    and used to diminish.

For all who have been there
    (or for wherever you have been),
I offer this blessing
    as a bright crimson cord
    to disrupt destruction:

When you are pushed to edges,
    may you insist on your own story with such grit and grace
    that they have no choice but to tell it.

When you are far from center,
    may you know the power and freedom
    that God grants to those on the margins.

When you face impossible choices,
    may you act with integrity and courage,
    resting in the shield of God's grace.

When others dismiss you with a label,
    may you claim your deep identity
    as a beloved child of the Creator.

RUTH

December 7

RUTH TRAVELS

READ:
Ruth 1:1–18

REFLECT:
In these opening verses of Ruth, it is not the command of God or a deep sense of piety and obedience that compels the characters, but basic hunger, a physical need for food. Because of the "famine in the land," Elimelech takes his family from their home in Bethlehem (which, ironically, means "house of bread") to the foreign territory of Moab.

This is not the first mention of Moab in Scripture. Deuteronomy 23:3–6 says that no Moabite "shall be admitted to the assembly of the LORD," and that Israelites should not promote the "welfare" or "prosperity" of Moabites. Yet in the midst of a famine, Elimelech and Naomi readily travel the fifty miles from Bethlehem to Moab in an effort to feed themselves and their children.

This journey meant to save the family, however, results in the deaths of the three men: first Elimelech, and then, about ten years later, Elimelech and Naomi's sons Mahlon and Chilion. As with Tamar's husband and brother-in-law, the circumstances of the deaths are irrelevant to the story; the fact of their deaths clears the way for the women to act on their own and make key decisions to ensure their survival and the continuation of the family line.

Naomi does just that. She recognizes that Moab is not a good place for her—particularly not as a widow with no sons or grandsons. She has heard that there is once again bread in Bethlehem, so she plans to move back home. Both of her daughters-in-law begin the journey with her, but Naomi soon tells them to return to their own mothers.

In Naomi's mind, her only value to Ruth and Orpah is her ability to provide husbands for them. Since she is no longer able to bear children, she believes that she has nothing to offer. Orpah, reluctantly, returns home, but Ruth insists on staying with Naomi. Emotion-laden verbs dominate this scene: *wept, kissed, clung*. Ruth's words to Naomi have been read in countless weddings:

Where you go, I will go;
where you lodge, I will lodge;
your people shall be my people,
and your God my God. (Ruth 1:16)

While basic human hunger compels Naomi's family from Bethlehem to Moab in the beginning of the story, a different motivation prompts Ruth's journey from Moab to Bethlehem. Her exact motive, though, is not fully revealed. Perhaps Ruth, for any number of reasons, does not want to return to her mother's house. Maybe she feels the need to put some physical distance between herself and the location of her deep grief of widowhood and childlessness. Or, as her impassioned speech certainly suggests, maybe she and Naomi have developed a deep bond that Ruth cannot bear to break. While fifty miles is a short distance for us today, for these women it meant almost a week's travel. If Ruth stays in Moab, she will likely never see Naomi again.

Whatever her reasons, Ruth clings to Naomi and insists on traveling with her to Judah. Naomi relents, and the two women travel on together to the sacred city of Bethlehem—a city that plays such an important role in our Christmas narratives.

Ruth's decision to go with Naomi to Bethlehem reminds us that saying yes to one journey—whether it involves literal geographical travel or more metaphorical movement as we embark on a new course of study, a new job, a new relationship, a new project—always means saying no to many other possibilities. And we almost always have to make our decision—about whether to stay or go, about which road to take, about whom we will travel with—before we know fully what the outcome of that decision will be.

Without knowing where any given path will take us, we make our decisions based on myriad factors: ease, convenience, fear, avoidance, hope, adventure, advice, previous experience. In the end, it is Ruth's love for Naomi that compels her to go to Bethlehem. May we all, on our own journeys, be compelled by such love.

CONNECT:

Look through photos of a trip that you have taken. Think about why you went, who went with you, and what the experience was like.

CONSIDER:

In the past, what has prompted you to leave the comfortable for the unknown? What journey—literal or metaphorical—are you on right now? Whom do you choose to accompany you? What is your emptiness, and where—or how—do you think you can fill it? What are you willing to risk to find fullness?

December 8

RUTH SUPPORTS NAOMI

READ:
Ruth 1:19–2:7

REFLECT:
The narrator makes it clear that Ruth returns with Naomi to Bethlehem, but you wouldn't know it by listening to Naomi. She speaks only of herself and the bitter way God has dealt with her. There is not even a mention of Ruth—no introductions, no sign of gratitude for her daughter-in-law who has made the long journey with her.

Naomi's entire speech is full of negativity and self-pity. She insists her name be changed from "pleasant" to "bitter." She idealizes the past in Bethlehem, saying she went away full, when in actuality she left because of a famine. She claims she is returning empty, when in fact Ruth is with her and the two women seem to be in good health. She insists that God has brought calamity to her, even though she has just returned home safely.

This is clearly a woman in grief, with the deaths of her husband and sons looming so large in her life that she cannot recognize or acknowledge any positive realities. It's not surprising that "the women" who greet Naomi upon her return to Bethlehem disappear after this speech. Who would want to listen to this constant negativity? We don't hear from the women again until the birth of Obed at the very end of the book.

Is it possible that Ruth insisted on accompanying Naomi because she realized what a fragile state Naomi was in? It is difficult to imagine what would have become of Naomi if she had arrived in Bethlehem alone. She doesn't seem to be able to relate well to people or figure out a way to support herself. Naomi doesn't even mention her husband's rich relative or seek out his support.

It is Ruth who takes action by going to the fields to glean. And whether through her own investigation or by luck, Ruth ends up in the field of Boaz, the prominent rich kinsman that Naomi neglected to mention. Ruth works hard enough in the fields to impress the servant, who tells Boaz about her.

Yet apparently, even though the servant is impressed, he can't be bothered with Ruth's name; she is "the Moabite who came back with Naomi." In this story about Ruth in a book named after her, only the narrator calls her by name. The people surrounding Ruth identify her by her nationality and relationship to Naomi.

Ruth, however, seems unconcerned about how others perceive her. She does not seem resentful of Naomi's neglect, but rather finds a way to help provide for her mother-in-law. She does not seek any special treatment in the fields. Ruth does what she thinks is best to do—what she believes needs to be done—regardless of how other people perceive her.

Of all Ruth's virtues, perhaps this is the most impressive. We all long for acknowledgment, recognition, gratitude. For people to call us by name and introduce us to their friends. And too often, perhaps, we let people's dismissiveness, their lack of gratitude, affect our actions. The holidays can be an especially sensitive time, when we may be doing a lot for others with little recognition, when we may interact more intensely with friends and family who do not give us proper respect or appreciation. Ruth's example encourages us to make choices based on our best sense of what is good and right, regardless of how others treat us in the process.

In addition to Ruth's positive example here, we should also pay attention to the negative examples of Naomi, "the women," the servant, and all those in Bethlehem who fail to properly acknowledge this foreigner in their midst. The busyness and stress of the holidays can cause us to neglect people around us. So Naomi and the others can encourage us to offer the acknowledgment, recognition, and gratitude that those around us deserve. As you go through your day, perhaps you want to make an effort to call people by name, engage them in meaningful conversation, and say thank you at every opportunity.

CONNECT:
Write a thank you note to someone whose presence you feel you have taken for granted recently.

CONSIDER:
When have you felt that your presence and efforts were not appreciated? Did people's lack of appreciation affect your actions? When have you felt dismissed? How did you respond? What helps you let go of the need for recognition and acknowledgment?

December 9

RUTH CARES FOR HERSELF

READ:
Ruth 2:8–23

REFLECT:
"May the LORD reward you for your deeds" (Ruth 2:12). In these first words that Boaz speaks to Ruth, we see that he appreciates the sacrifices Ruth has made in leaving her family to travel to this foreign land. With these words, Boaz invokes divine blessing and protection for Ruth, but she has something more concrete and earthly in mind. She responds: "May I continue to find favor in your sight, my lord" (v. 13). Where Boaz refers to "the LORD," Ruth appeals to "my lord." There is no indication that Ruth rejects the God of the people in this new land, but she also recognizes the power that the people around her have to make her life easier or more difficult.

Boaz's kindness to Ruth continues when he invites her to join him and his reapers at the table for mealtime. He is abundantly generous, heaping food on her plate, giving her even more than she can eat. He does not provide only this one meal, though. Boaz gives instructions to his reapers to ensure that Ruth will be able to glean plenty of grain so that she and Naomi will continue to have food.

These instructions seem to be given to the reapers after Ruth has left the table, and I wonder whether she realizes this additional kindness from Boaz. Does she suspect that the men are pulling out extra handfuls of grain from their bundles and leaving them for her to glean? Or does she just think that Boaz has particularly careless people working for him?

In any case, Ruth returns home to Naomi that evening with a large amount of grain. Notice, though, this important line: "Then [Ruth] took out and gave [Naomi] what was left over after she herself had been satisfied" (v. 18). While Boaz spoke of all that Ruth had sacrificed for Naomi, we see here that Ruth is tending to her own needs. She does not neglect herself even as she works to provide for Naomi as well.

Ruth is often held up as a virtuous woman, but her practice of self-care is not a virtue that is often highlighted—maybe because it is not a virtue that is generally affirmed or appreciated among Christians in general, and Christian women in particular. We are more likely to hear of Ruth's other virtues: her loyalty, her hard work, her generosity, even her bravery in going to a foreign land. But in all my years of hearing about Ruth, nobody has ever pointed out that Ruth satisfied herself before giving Naomi the leftovers.

It may feel uncomfortable to consider caring for ourselves as a Christian virtue. My childhood church had a Sunday school class called JOY: "Jesus first, others second, yourself last." And regardless of whether a church offers a class with such a name, the general message of self-denial is communicated pretty clearly in many, many churches. But if Ruth is, indeed, a hero of the faith to emulate, then we need to take the virtue of self-care seriously.

Note, also, that self-care is not selfishness. Ruth "satisfies" herself, but she also gives plenty of grain to Naomi. And it is precisely Ruth's care for herself that gives her the ability to spend days in the fields gleaning and providing for both herself and Naomi.

The holidays can be a time when we are called upon to give much to many people. We give time for holiday events, money for gifts, emotional energy for people who are struggling. Amid the busyness, we need to feed ourselves so that we have energy and strength to also tend to the people around us.

CONNECT:
Do something for yourself today that will "satisfy" you and bring you joy.

CONSIDER:
How do you feel about considering self-care a virtue? Have you known someone (or been someone) who experienced negative consequences because they gave too much to others and failed to care for themselves? Have you known (or been) someone who uses "self-care" as an excuse to neglect the needs of others? How can you find the virtuous space of caring for yourself and for those around you?

December 10

RUTH GOES TO BOAZ

READ:
Ruth 3

REFLECT:
Now that the harvest is over, Naomi realizes that she and Ruth need to establish a more permanent form of security other than sending Ruth out to glean in the fields. So she gives Ruth some rather shocking instructions: get dressed up, go hide on Boaz's threshing floor, and then, when Boaz lies down, uncover his "feet" (a euphemism for genitals) and lie down with him.

It's a bold plan, and Ruth does not hesitate to carry it out. She is "stealthy" as she climbs into bed with the sleeping Boaz, and when he wakes up and sees her there, she tells him to "spread [his] cloak" over her (Ruth 3:9). The sexual implications of this scene are unmistakable. Ruth, following Naomi's instructions, intends to lead Boaz to marry her through this act of seduction.

Perhaps you recognize this setup from the story of Tamar: a widow seeks security through the seduction of a man related to her deceased husband. When Judah learns of Tamar's pregnancy, he orders her to be killed; but once he discovers that he is the one who has fathered the baby, he says that Tamar was right in her actions. Likewise, Boaz is startled to wake up in the middle of the night and discover a woman in bed with him. But once she says, "I am Ruth," Boaz commends her for her attempted seduction. As far as he is concerned, her willingness to marry him is a greater act of loyalty to Naomi than her initial travel to Bethlehem.

It is unclear exactly what happens between Ruth and Boaz on the threshing floor, but it is clear that Ruth's presence there that night motivates Boaz to take immediate steps toward marrying her. As she prepares to leave early the next morning, Boaz gives her six measures of barley. During the harvest, Boaz provided for Ruth indirectly by instructing his workers to leave grain for her to glean. Now Boaz gives her the food directly, already treating her as a family member rather than a stranger.

It may feel uncomfortable to have acts of sexual seduction and trickery at the heart of two of the five stories of the women in Jesus' genealogy. And it may seem surprising, by churchy standards, that the women are not condemned but rather praised for their seduction. The focus of the praise, of course, is not about the sex, but about the willingness of the women to take action on their own behalf, to work against the limitations that society put on them because of their status as women and as widows.

How often do we choose not to take action because we are afraid someone will disapprove, that we will get "in trouble"? This can happen when we want to take steps toward our own security and prosperity; people might think we are selfish or privileged or presumptuous or just foolish. It also happens when we want to speak out and act on behalf of other—particularly marginalized—people; we might be seen as judgmental or too political or uninformed or difficult.

It is true that the responses of Judah and Boaz to the bold actions of Tamar and Ruth are best-case scenarios. People do not always appreciate it when we do what we feel needs to be done. Still, the story of Ruth can give us confidence to step out and take risks in advocating for ourselves and for others.

CONNECT:

Think of someone you know (or know of) who has taken action despite the threat of other people's disapproval. Offer a prayer of thanks for that person. Write their name on a piece of paper that you can carry with you, and pray for them throughout the day.

CONSIDER:

What is one thing you have been hesitant to do because you fear how other people might react? What is the best-case scenario if you take the risk and do the thing? What is a possible negative outcome if you take the risk? Where do you sense God leading you?

December 11

RUTH IS SILENCED

READ:
Ruth 4:1–12

REFLECT:
Ruth's conversation with Naomi at the end of chapter 3 is the last we hear from her in this book of the Bible that bears her name. The action shifts now from Ruth and Naomi to Boaz and the men at the gate. Along with the acquisition of land, Boaz also negotiates with the next-of-kin regarding the acquisition of Ruth, who is presented as a problematic piece of property.

Once the land and wife deal is formalized by exchanging sandals, the men who have served as witnesses to the agreement offer a blessing: "May the LORD make the woman who is coming into your house like Rachel and Leah, who together built up the house of Israel" (Ruth 4:11). It is surprising that these Israelite men would compare Ruth, a foreigner from the disparaged country of Moab, to Rachel and Leah, two prominent ancestors of the Jewish faith. It seems that Ruth's actions and her imminent marriage to Boaz have shifted her status in the community, allowing her to be considered part of the group rather than an outsider.

The blessing concludes, "May your house be like the house of Perez, whom Tamar bore to Judah" (v. 12). Considering the similarities we've already noted between Ruth and Tamar, it is interesting that Tamar's name would come up here. Notice that Perez is identified as a son Tamar bore to Judah, when the whole point of Tamar seducing Judah was to bear a son for her deceased husband Er. So while Tamar's actions were intended to carry on the name of her first husband, it is ultimately her own name that is perpetuated and shared through the generations because of the birth of Perez. The same can be said for Ruth. In theory, Boaz is allowing Ruth to carry on the name of her deceased husband. In reality, Ruth and Boaz are the ones named in the genealogy of Jesus, and Ruth is the one whose name carries on through the biblical book bearing her name.

Considering Ruth's prominence in the story, her sudden transition from subject to object here in chapter 4 is rather disconcerting. Yet even as her voice is removed from her own story, she is lifted up by the men at the gate and given a place in the broader story of the Israelite people.

As frustrating as it can be, we are not always in charge of our own stories. There are situations where others make important decisions that will profoundly affect our lives. There are times when our status in a group hangs on the words of those with more standing; where our acceptance or rejection depends on factors beyond our control.

In earlier conversations that Ruth has with both Boaz and Naomi, her conversation partners claim that blessings come from God, while Ruth herself seems to attribute positive events—such as having enough grain—to the actions of the people around her. Ruth, remember, is from Moab and did not grow up believing in the God of the Israelites. She is still learning and growing in her faith and her understanding of God.

And perhaps from this marginalized perspective, Ruth brings an important reality into the discussion; perhaps the blessings come both from God *and* from the kindness, the wisdom, the help of people around us. Church people can sometimes be dismissive of secular Christmas festivities, insisting that we remember that "Jesus is the reason for the season." And certainly, as people of faith, we want to keep the story of the incarnation at the heart of all we do—in December and all year long. It is also true that "secular" Christmas celebrations can be helpful and meaningful in their own ways: bringing people together, supporting people in need, offering joy and encouragement during what (in the Northern Hemisphere) is otherwise a pretty dreary season. Amid these holidays and holy days, we can receive blessings from God and from the people around us.

Ruth's story shows us that when we are not at the table—or the gate—when decisions are being made that affect us, we can trust in God *and* in the goodness of others. Unfortunately, others will not always make decisions that are for our good; in these times we can call on our faith and seek to continue to trust in God's goodness.

Of course, we are not always the one on the margins. There are times when we might find ourselves in a position of talking about and making decisions that will deeply affect people who are not part of the conversation. In those moments, we can trust in the grace of God *and* we can use our position and power to advocate for those who are not present, and maybe even invite them to the table. Nobody deserves to be written out of their own story.

CONNECT:

In today's reading, Ruth is connected to Leah, Rachel, and Tamar. Think about which of your ancestors you are most like. Look through some old family photos if you have them. Thank God for those who have gone before, and pray that you can be a support and blessing for those who come after.

CONSIDER:

Think about a time when you were not consulted about a decision that directly affected you. How did that feel? What did you do? When have you been in a position to make decisions that directly affect the lives of others? How might you more fully include others in decisions that will affect them?

December 12

RUTH GIVES BIRTH

READ:
Ruth 4:13–22

REFLECT:
Ruth is once again a wife instead of a widow. This has been the hope, the goal, from the beginning: that she would "find security . . . in the house of [her] husband" (Ruth 1:9). While her ten-year marriage to Mahlon produced no children, Ruth becomes pregnant very soon after marrying Boaz.

For a woman to bear a son, particularly in Ruth's cultural context, should bring her significant honor and standing in the community, but in this case, Ruth disappears after she gives birth. It is not Ruth but Naomi whom "the women" congratulate on the birth. These women name him Obed and proclaim: "A son has been born to Naomi" (Ruth 4:17). And it is Naomi who, somehow, nurses the child. While Ruth is named in the genealogy of Jesus, she is not named here, at the end of her own book of the Bible, in the genealogy of her great-grandson David.

In one sense, Ruth's disappearance seems like a slight. She is not even given credit and honor for the son whom she bears and births. Yet it is very interesting to me that Ruth is not presented as a mother. Yes, it says that Ruth "bore a son" (v. 13), but beyond that, Naomi is in the role of Obed's mother, which allows Ruth to be thought of primarily in the context of her earlier actions: traveling to a foreign land with her mother-in-law, providing food for her household, boldly securing a future for both herself and Naomi.

The women tell Naomi that Ruth is more to her "than seven sons" (v. 15). This statement gives Ruth value and honor well beyond her role as Obed's mother. Having seven sons would mean that Naomi would never have to worry about having food to eat or a place to live. Seven sons could ensure a family line for generations upon generations to come. Seven sons would almost certainly guarantee that Naomi's name and memory would be honored throughout the generations. Ruth does, indeed, provide all this for her mother-in-law. So by de-emphasizing Ruth's role as mother, her significance as a "son" is highlighted and appreciated. In fulfilling this traditionally masculine role, then, it makes sense that Ruth would be listed in Jesus' genealogy.

As we consider Ruth's significance to the family line of Jesus, we should take particular note of what the women say to Naomi: they say that Ruth loves her. I wonder what they have seen between the two women that causes them to make this statement. Is it simply Ruth's loyalty? Do the women attribute Ruth's willingness to leave home, her hard work gleaning in the fields, and her marriage to Naomi's next of kin as acts of love? Or is there more? Have the women observed something in the way Ruth and Naomi look at each other, speak to each other, form a household together, that leads them to understand that there is love between the two women?

In the end, perhaps it is love—in any number of forms—that is the important thing. Not who gets the credit or whose name goes on the list. Not the roles that people put us in or even the roles we claim for ourselves. But simply the fact of our love for others, and the way that love shows up in the world.

Our lives, like Ruth's, can hold a lot of grief and a lot of fear. We may be faced with difficult decisions and be called upon to take great risks. We may need to work hard and receive little acknowledgment for it all. There are layers that can feel complicated and disorienting. And yet there is, in the midst and at the core, the sustaining, guiding reality of love.

CONNECT:

Engage in the practice of *visio divina* with the image that accompanies tomorrow's blessing. First, get in a comfortable position with the image in your line of sight. Take a few deep breaths and invite the Holy Spirit to guide your reflection. Next, let your focus settle on whichever part of the image draws your attention. What thoughts or emotions come to mind as you focus on that one part of the image? Next, pull your gaze back to include the entire image. What other aspects of the image do you notice? How does the image, as a whole, make you feel? Do you sense any word from the Holy Spirit as you sit and pray with this image?

CONSIDER:

Where is your love most evident in the world? Whom would people say that you love? How can they tell? In what ways does your love for others sustain you? How can you allow love to more fully guide your words and actions?

December 13

RUTH'S BLESSING

Dear friend,
  we will face deep disappointment
  and unbearable grief.
Emptiness will taunt us.
Hunger will gnaw.
It will seem impossible to travel to the unknown land,
  and more impossible to go back to the fatally familiar.

But oh, dear friend,
  we will also be startled by beauty
  and catch glimpses of joy.
Contentment will sneak up on us.
Abundance will delight.
We will realize that
  while the entire journey is impossible,
  the next step is not.
Nor is the next.

So for each step you take toward that foreign land of home,
I offer this blessing to kiss and to cling to:
May you have courage
  to leave where you've been,
  to travel to where you're going,
  and to do what needs to be done when you get there.
May you have indifference
  about how much credit you get,

how many times they say thank you,
and whether or not they call you by name.
May you have wisdom
in the work you choose,
the roles you fill,
and the generosity you exhibit.
And through it all—
in and around and under and above it all—
may you be guided by love.

BATHSHEBA

"The Wife of Uriah"

December 14

BATHSHEBA SUFFERS AN ASSAULT

READ:
2 Samuel 11:1–5

REFLECT:
This is a difficult story, friends. I wish it didn't exist in Scripture at all, especially not as part of the story of Jesus' ancestors. And I really wish this were not a story that continues to be all too familiar today: people using their power to sexually assault someone and then avoid the consequences of their bad behavior.

There's a lot to say about King David in this passage: how cowardly and entitled he is to be home napping while "all Israel" is on the battlefield; how he finds out Bathsheba is married and then sends for her anyway; how he already has six wives available to him; how easily he dismisses Bathsheba after he rapes her.

Yes, there is *a lot* to say about David here. It's more difficult to figure out what's going on with Bathsheba. While she likely took some action and spoke some words, the narrator presents her as passive. Which is how rape stories generally go when being told on behalf of the rapist. The woman wanted sex. Or if she didn't want it, she at least didn't mind. Or if she did mind, she didn't say anything, so how's a guy to know?

Without having any details of the sexual encounter, many people hesitate to label this a rape. But anyone who has received any training for healthy boundaries or sexual assault prevention can see right away that Bathsheba's "lying with" David is strongly coerced, if not outright forced.

The NRSV translation says that "David sent messengers to get her," but several other translations (AMP, ASV, ESV, MEV) say that the messengers "took her" (2 Samuel 11:4). However we translate the verb, it's clear that when the king's men show up at her door, Bathsheba does not really have a choice about whether she will go with them. And when they take her to King David, regardless of how much force he may or may not use, how much she may or may not protest, she really does not have a choice about whether he has sex with her. The power differential is too great—physically, politically, socially—for Bathsheba to do anything other than comply.

The narrator of this story relates only two uncoerced actions that Bathsheba takes here. First, she bathes. We don't know where she is bathing, only that David can see her from his roof. Presumably the king would have a taller house than other people, and thus a good vantage point from which to see many of the activities going on in the neighborhood. I imagine he could see into walled courtyards and other areas that people on the ground would consider private spaces. So the fact that David can see Bathsheba bathing does not suggest she intends to make herself sexually available.

The other action Bathsheba takes is to send word to David about her pregnancy. If Bathsheba is discovered to have become pregnant while her husband was away, she could be executed for adultery. So in contacting the king, Bathsheba seeks to hold him accountable for his actions; she sets up an expectation that he will take action to address this difficult situation he has created. She cannot know how David will respond to the message she sends, but in contrast to David's subsequent acts of deceit, she chooses to engage the situation with openness and honesty.

Both Bathsheba's presumed nakedness as she bathes and her honesty about her pregnancy suggest that, both before and after David rapes her, she is a truthful woman with nothing to hide or be ashamed of. From a societal point of view, David is the one with power in this situation as Bathsheba waits for David to respond to her message.

During Advent, as we consider the story of Jesus' birth, we know that about a thousand years after David, there was another king, Herod, who also used lies and manipulation to get what he wanted and protect his power. Even as we focus on Bathsheba's strength, on the joy of Jesus' birth, on the bright spots then and in our world today, David and Herod and so many other "kings" loom in the background. There are plenty of people who would use their power to protect themselves while endangering others, to compel people to do things, to grasp for more and more—power, money, sex—when they already have more than enough.

When we read the full story of David and Bathsheba, of Jesus and Herod, it turns out that goodness and honesty, vulnerability and openness, can actually win out over self-centered forms of power. But we aren't yet through the full story. We are here, with Bathsheba, after she has sent news of her pregnancy to her very powerful rapist.

This isn't where we want to be, but sometimes it's where we are. Sometimes it's the only place we can be. *Present*. Present with ourselves in our own trauma and violations. Present with others who have experienced trauma. And as we are present we know that God, through the vulnerability of Jesus, is present with us as well.

CONNECT:
Be gentle with yourself today. Breathe deeply. Seek beauty.

CONSIDER:

When have you been present with someone else during a time of grief and trauma? When has someone been present with you in a difficult time? What helps you sense God's presence when you experience difficult feelings?

December 15

BATHSHEBA LAMENTS

READ:
2 Samuel 11:6–11, 14–15, 26–27

REFLECT:
After yesterday's story of rape, you were probably hoping for something a little more cheery today. Unfortunately, as is so often the case, one act of harm leads to another. In an attempt to deal with the "problem" of Bathsheba's pregnancy, David decides to bring her husband Uriah home from battle so that Bathsheba can have sex with her husband and everyone can pretend the baby is his.

Of course, David's plan does not work out, because Uriah does something David, apparently, could not imagine: he refuses to enjoy the comforts of his home while his fellow soldiers remain on the battlefield. When David learns that Uriah has not, in fact, slept with Bathsheba, he instructs his military commander, Joab, to place Uriah on the front lines of battle and to draw back when the enemy attacks him. There are so many terrible things about this—the request itself, of course, which constitutes murder; the fact that David is using Uriah's virtue against him; the fact that David sends this note *with Uriah*; and the terrible position in which this request puts Joab.

But David is a powerful man. Uriah delivers the note, oblivious to its contents, and Joab complies, ensuring Uriah's death.

Through all this, it seems, Bathsheba is waiting at home to see how David will respond to the news of her pregnancy. Did she even know her husband was briefly in town? If so, did she suspect David's intent? We don't know how much she knows or how she feels about David's scheming. We only know that when she hears that her husband is dead, she goes into mourning. On top of the trauma of rape and pregnancy, Bathsheba now bears the grief of her husband's death—actually, his murder, which she surely recognized.

In yesterday's portion of the story, Bathsheba took two actions: bathing, and notifying David of her pregnancy. Here she takes only one action: to make "lamentation" (2 Samuel 11:26). She actively mourns the death of her husband. And then, when the mourning period is over, she is once again an object for David to have brought to him, for David to marry, for David to impregnate.

In one sense, the narrator's refusal to grant Bathsheba agency is maddening, but in another sense, the presentation of the situation in this way ensures that the blame rests squarely on David. For those who would read this story and blame Bathsheba for being raped ("Just look at what she was wearing!") and accuse her of committing adultery in a plot to gain a position in the royal household, we have this clarifying comment from the narrator: "The thing that David had done displeased the LORD" (v. 27). The rape, the deception, the murder—this is all David's doing. Bathsheba is moved around at David's whim, and she suffers terrible consequences from his actions.

When bad things happen to us, when tragedies occur, we naturally ask why. We want someone to blame. We want to understand a reason so that we can keep the bad thing from happening again. Sometimes we are quick to blame ourselves, to note all our failings, all the things we could have or should have done differently: If I had bathed in a different place; if I had told the king's men no; if I had gone to the entrance of the king's house and dragged Uriah home with me; if . . . if . . . if . . .

Of course, sometimes we do make mistakes. Our actions—or inactions—cause harm to ourselves and to others. We have to be honest about that, to name the sin and seek forgiveness. But those who are most deeply wounded by others often take on more blame than is their due. They don't fully assess the power dynamics. They overestimate what effect they could have had in a particular situation. It's hard to imagine anything Bathsheba could have done to counteract the will of King David in this story.

During Advent, as we await the One who forgives our sins, perhaps it is a good time to consider what responsibilities we bear and what guilt we need to release, what power we truly hold and what powers we cannot control.

CONNECT:
Talk to God (out loud, silently, or in writing) about a situation where you experienced harm or one where you feel you caused harm. Ask God for clarity about the power dynamics involved, ask for forgiveness if you need it, and ask for peace in moving forward.

CONSIDER:
What is the difference between healthy use of power and abusive use of power? Where do you see power being used in abusive ways—among people you know or in the world at large? Whom do you see using power in healthy ways? As followers of Jesus, how are we called to use power?

December 16

BATHSHEBA GRIEVES

READ:
2 Samuel 12:15b–24

REFLECT:
The death of Bathsheba's child—who we assume is her firstborn—
layers one more trauma on top of all the other trauma she has
experienced. Bathsheba endures seven days of gut-wrenching dread;
seven days of trying to care for a sick baby who is wailing, whining,
feverish, not sleeping enough or sleeping too much. I'm sure she
nursed him and swaddled him, rocked him and bounced him. In the
end, none of it was enough. While Bathsheba tends to the sick child
and David lies on the ground, fasting and praying, the baby dies.

We know that David responds to the child's death by worshiping God and eating a hearty meal—which is not a bad response. In
fact, it's what we still tend to do—church folks often serve a nice
meal after a funeral. We know less about Bathsheba's reaction to the
death. We only know that she needs to be consoled.

The way the story is presented, it seems like David goes to Bathsheba shortly after the child's death, and that in consoling her he
also has sex with her—which seems problematic in a few ways. Even
aside from the ritual purity issues involved (see Leviticus 12:1–5), it
is medically ill-advised for a woman to have sexual intercourse so
soon after giving birth. Emotionally, it's difficult to say how Bathsheba might feel about such an encounter; David is her husband
now, and also someone who committed a sexual assault against her.

The narration implies that this sexual encounter results in Bathsheba's becoming pregnant again. Which seems highly unlikely from a biological standpoint, and terribly ill-advised for Bathsheba's mental and physical health. More likely than Bathsheba becoming pregnant immediately after her infant dies is that the narrator is conflating a longer period of time here, ignoring the natural rhythm of women's cycles to speed up the story of the king and his heirs.

It strikes me how very much this story centers on David, even though Bathsheba is the one who carries the child, gives birth to him, nurses him, cares for him, and bears his loss in her body. The narrator tries to center David's story, but it is obvious for anyone paying attention that Bathsheba is actually at the center.

Likewise, the narrator strings actions together to account for what David needs—a new heir—while completely neglecting the biological realities of conception and childbearing. It turns out that the narrator can, in fact, tell the story however he wants. It is also true that Bathsheba's body was undoubtedly in charge of the timeline here. David may be in a hurry to have another son, but he cannot force Bathsheba's body to conceive before it is ready.

Isn't that part of what the season of Advent is about? Spending time we don't think we have. Waiting for something we wish would happen right away. Being forced into a timeline not of our own making.

While menstrual cycles tend to be more obvious and recognized, *all* human bodies experience cycles. Our hormones, and thus our moods, ebb and flow. Our bodies experience changes—subtle and not so subtle with daily, monthly, or seasonal cycles and as the years progress. We want to construct our own stories, but sometimes we are simply not in charge of the timeline. However close we shove the sentences together when we tell the story, some things, in real life, take time.

Advent is an invitation to live in real time, to stop trying to bridge the gaps and simply live in them instead.

CONNECT:

Read Genesis 1:14–19. Look up when the next full moon and the next new moon will be. Mark those dates on your calendar, and as they come, give thanks to God for the divine rhythms established in creation.

CONSIDER:

How does your body experience daily, monthly, or seasonal cycles or the natural process of aging? What frustrates you about these physical rhythms? What do you appreciate? How can you celebrate the beauty of your body, which is created by God?

December 17

BATHSHEBA APPROACHES KING DAVID

READ:
1 Kings 1:11–31

REFLECT:
Many years have passed since our last reading. Bathsheba's second baby, Solomon, is now a grown man; the powerful king, David, is now an old and ailing man; and the once silent, passive Bathsheba is now a bold, powerful woman.

She is, apparently, a confidant of the prophet Nathan, who has been a close, trusted advisor of David. Following Nathan's advice, but of her own volition, she goes to David to advocate for her son Solomon and his right to the throne. She reminds David of the promise he made to her: that Solomon would succeed David as king. The interesting thing is, there is no record in Scripture of David making such a promise to Bathsheba. (First Chronicles 29 does indicate that David intends Solomon to be his successor, but Bathsheba is not present and the text relates quite a different story of how Solomon comes to power.)

Perhaps David *has* promised Bathsheba that her son will take the throne. (Given David's previous actions, we can imagine he might have promised *all kinds* of things to all kinds of people.) Or perhaps David never made any such promise and Bathsheba is trying to convince him that he did. Either way, Bathsheba is bold to go before the king and ask him to tell the people that Solomon should succeed him. For the most part, David seems to listen to the prophet Nathan, but for some reason Nathan thinks it best for Bathsheba to go to David first. As a court insider, Nathan perceives that Bathsheba holds some degree of influence over the king.

Bathsheba goes to David as a mother and makes a request for her beloved child—this second son she bore, the one who lived. It would be expected that she would go to the king on behalf of her son, not herself. Yet it is clear that Solomon's fate and her own are closely linked. If Adonijah's kingship is allowed to stand, she insists that both "Solomon and I will be counted offenders" (1 Kings 1:21). She clearly understands that in promoting her son's position and power, she is also promoting her own.

In this passage, Bathsheba exercises power, but within acceptable confines. She goes to the king only because of the counsel of Nathan. She speaks primarily (whether truthful or not) of what the king himself has said, not of her own desires. And she is there on behalf of her son, not herself. Bathsheba is bold. She is also wise. She knows the rules, and she follows them.

This story of Bathsheba, along with the Christmas story, can help us think about how we confront power. In the birth of Jesus, God enters the world as a human infant—a move that is both bold and vulnerable, much like Bathsheba approaching the throne of David. Such boldness is commendable. Like Bathsheba, we must be willing to take a risk in approaching those with power over us. But along with the boldness, we must also be wise. It is good to get counsel from someone with insight, someone who is on the inside and knows the system. And in our boldness and wisdom, we must also recognize our vulnerability. Confronting power always comes with risks, risks we may be called to take on behalf of those we love and on behalf of those who are even more vulnerable than we are.

CONNECT:

Call or write to someone who holds a position of power regarding an issue you care about. You might contact an elected official, your boss, or even your pastor.

CONSIDER:

When have you made a request to someone in power? What wisdom did you seek before making your request? What risks did you take? How did it work out? Is there anything you would like to do differently next time?

December 18

BATHSHEBA APPROACHES
KING SOLOMON

READ:
1 Kings 2:13–25

REFLECT:
The Bathsheba we encounter in 1 Kings is quite different from the one we met in 2 Samuel.

Bathsheba, the sexual assault victim and widow, is now Bathsheba, the queen mother. In her role as King Solomon's mother, Bathsheba is in a unique position of influence over the most powerful man in Israel. We sense her power when Adonijah approaches Bathsheba and asks her to go to the king with a request. And her power is confirmed by the throne that Solomon has brought in for her.

Adonijah wants Bathsheba to use her power to make Abishag his wife. Last we saw Abishag, she was "attending" King David. While her relationship with David was not sexual—presumably because David's age and illness made him impotent—it was clearly intimate (see 1 Kings 1:3–4). We assume that Solomon "inherited" Abishag when David died, and now Adonijah wants Solomon to "give" her to him.

Here, as in Ruth, it is upsetting to see a woman treated as a piece of property to be negotiated and traded among men. Bathsheba's attempt to facilitate the requested "transaction" is particularly disturbing, because Bathsheba knows what it is like to be treated as property, to be taken by a man because he believes he has a right to her body. We want to see Bathsheba, as a woman, use her position of power to protect other women; maybe even to change the way women are treated.

But that's probably an unfair expectation, because Bathsheba is not a *universal* woman; she is a particular woman. All the experiences and relationships of her life form who she is and the decisions she makes. She is not speaking with Adonijah as "a woman," but as Bathsheba. She does not go to Solomon as a representative of her gender, but as the mother of the king. She may have her own reasons for taking this request to Solomon: revenge on the woman who has had a too-intimate relationship with her husband; an attempt to facilitate Adonijah's death; a sincere effort to create peace between the brothers.

The truth is, while we know a little bit about what Bathsheba does, we know nothing about her interior life. We don't know her fears, her hopes, her motivations. There's a way to read her story that places her in the role of victim. There's a way to read her story that frames her as a woman who manipulates men for her own purposes and pleasure. There's a way to read her story—probably the more faithful way—that understands her as a complex person struggling to find her way in a world that grants her, at first, almost no power and then, somehow, almost too much.

Power can be insidious. Sometimes we use our power intentionally—for good or for ill. Often, we are hesitant to accept the fact that we have any power at all. If our power comes from long-held privilege of race, sex, or class, it can be nearly invisible to us. If we have been in positions of powerlessness in the past, we may not know what power feels like or how to handle it. We may think of power only in terms of David commanding his troops and may dismiss power that shows up as Bathsheba asking a favor of her son.

As we see from Bathsheba's full story—and from the world around us—power is complicated. The ways we use power affect many people, including ourselves.

Advent invites us to consider power in light of the incarnation. It is astounding to think that the all-powerful God becomes human and is born as a tiny, vulnerable baby. What kind of power is that?

CONNECT:

Make a list of the people you have power over—these may be specific names or groups of people. Pray for each of those people and ask God for the wisdom to use your power wisely.

CONSIDER:

What does the incarnation—the coming of God to the world in the person of Jesus—suggest about the nature of power? How do you think God exercises power in the world?

BATHSHEBA'S BLESSING

Nobody knows what to make of me.
Temptress or victim.
Bride or widow.
Queen or concubine.
Calculating or naive.

Siblings, listen:
People will write their own stories over your life—
    fill in their own motives,
    project their own fears,
    reach for their own dreams.
Your life—as it turns out—
    has very little to do with you.
At least how they tell it.
Which is why their story cannot be your guide;
    why you must bathe in your rooftop garden without guilt;
    why you must mourn your beloveds however you can;
    why you cannot believe the lie
    that their abuse was actually a favor
    to grant you a palace and a prince.

Even though my story is not well told,
    you know, at least, that I finally found a throne.
So from my royal seat,
    with whatever power it offers,

I bestow on you this blessing:
    for companions with integrity;
    for moments of delightful abandon;
    for love deep enough to cause grief;
    for consolation.
May you have the power that is your due
    and use that power on behalf of the vulnerable—
    even if the vulnerable one is you.
May you write your own story,
    and may it be told by compassionate voices
    in all generations to come.

MARY

December 20

MARY SAYS YES

READ:
Luke 1:26–38

REFLECT:
Did you notice the opening of this familiar passage? "In the sixth month the angel Gabriel was sent by God" (Luke 1:26). The sixth month of what? Well, if we back up the reading just a bit, we realize it is the sixth month of Elizabeth's pregnancy. The biblical narrator is tracking time according to a woman's reproductive cycle.

The writer of Luke continues to prioritize women's experience and identity in verse 29, which might be one of the most astounding verses in a quite astounding passage: "But [Mary] was much perplexed by [Gabriel's] words and pondered what sort of greeting this might be." Here we have a glimpse into the thoughts and emotions of a female biblical character. Mary is confused. She is analyzing the angel's words in her mind.

In all the other stories we have read up to this point—the stories of Tamar, Rahab, Ruth, and Bathsheba—we have been told only what the women *said* and what they *did*. We are never told how these women felt, what they thought, what their motivations were. Mary is being presented to us in a new way—as a fully formed person in her own right rather than simply an object that affects the male characters in some way.

The fact that Mary is humanized here—that she is given feelings, voice, and agency—is the saving grace of this story. Because the annunciation could otherwise be read as just another situation where a man (in this case, a masculine image of God) uses a woman for his own purposes; another instance of a woman's body being sacrificed to the whims of male desire. Mary's full humanity and agency are necessary for her true consent.

Mary does not ponder the angel's words only in her heart, though. After the angel tells her that she will conceive a son who will "reign over the house of Jacob forever" (v. 33), Mary ponders aloud. She asks Gabriel: "How can this be, since I am a virgin?" (v. 34). Can you imagine asking the angel Gabriel about sex? Mary could have asked so many other, less awkward questions: What do you mean my son will have David's throne? Can't this wait until Joseph and I are married? What if I want to name him Sam instead of Jesus?

Of all the questions to ask, Mary goes with what is, in many ways, the most basic question: How can I, as a virgin, get pregnant? I don't think I would have the presence of mind or self-assuredness to ask such a question of an angel visitor. And I'm not sure Gabriel was expecting such a question. Because his answer is a bit fuzzy. "The Holy Spirit will come upon you, and the power of the Most High will overshadow you" (v. 35). We often read and repeat these words as if they have some deep theological importance. And maybe they do. But it kind of sounds like Gabriel is just fumbling around trying to answer Mary's unanswerable question.

Still, as unsatisfying as that answer is, it is apparently enough for Mary. In all her confusion and wondering, in her pondering and questioning, she nevertheless gives her full consent: "Here am I, the servant of the Lord; let it be with me according to your word" (v. 38).

In this beautiful scene, we see that God welcomes all our questions. Indeed, it is only by asking questions that we can get to a place of fully consenting to—and therefore, fully participating in—the life that God is calling us to live. In Mary's response to Gabriel, we also see that even when we don't know what questions to ask, or when we don't fully understand the answers, God is faithful as we step into the mystery.

I wonder how I can be more like Mary—to enter into even the most incomprehensible situations wholeheartedly, but not naively; to be an enthusiastic participant with challenging questions; to speak my questions and proclaim my yes with equal authority and confidence.

CONNECT:

Consider an invitation you have received recently—perhaps a task someone has asked you to take on or a new role that has presented itself. Make a list of all the questions you have about this invitation. Talk with God about this invitation and see if God is leading you to an enthusiastic yes or a firm no.

CONSIDER:

Why do you think Mary says yes to God's plan? What reasons would she have had for saying no? How comfortable are you saying yes to situations where you don't know exactly what will happen? How comfortable are you asking questions of the people in charge before you say yes?

December 21

MARY VISITS ELIZABETH

READ:
Luke 1:39–45

REFLECT:
I think we need to take a moment here to acknowledge that the journey Mary takes from Nazareth to the Judean hill country was no quick, simple matter. We don't know exactly where Elizabeth lived, but it was probably at least an eighty-mile trip. Likely on foot. During the first trimester of Mary's pregnancy.

When I was pregnant, I had about a thirty-mile trip to work each day. By car. And I could show you the parking lot between my house and my job where I pulled over every morning to throw up. Traveling while pregnant is no picnic.

There's a lot we don't know about the journey Mary took. Did she go by herself? It seems strange that a young woman would take a three- to four-day journey alone, but nobody else is mentioned. (Maybe Mary figured she would be safe since she was carrying "the Son of the Most High.") Was Mary feeling sick? Were her ankles swollen? Did she have to stop and take a nap every afternoon?

Maybe more interesting than the *how* of the trip is the *why*. Why is visiting Elizabeth the first thing Mary wants to do after receiving news of her own pregnancy? Is it to congratulate Elizabeth? Is it to share her own news—and all the excitement and fear that go with it? Is it to get some practical advice and moral support for the physical difficulties of pregnancy? Or to ask Elizabeth's advice about what to tell Joseph? Whatever Mary expects to gain from this visit to Elizabeth, it is important enough for Mary to undertake an exhausting—and possibly dangerous—journey.

Maybe what Mary most needs from this trip is the blessing that Elizabeth offers: "Blessed are you among women, and blessed is the fruit of your womb" (Luke 1:42). Elizabeth serves a prophetic role here, recognizing the activity of God where others miss it. Mary might not yet be showing, but we can be sure that when others can tell she is pregnant, she will hear many words that are the opposite of blessing. As a pregnant, unwed teenager, Mary would have been shamed and shunned by many in her community. But Elizabeth, seemingly the first to know of the pregnancy, offers these words of blessing as a foundation for Mary's experience of motherhood.

And Elizabeth offers words of joy—so much joy—in a situation that will bring much difficulty and grief. We are told that Elizabeth's baby, John the Baptist, "leap[s] for joy" (v. 44) in her womb when Mary greets Elizabeth. And notice that Elizabeth blesses Mary twice. The second time, Elizabeth says, "Blessed is she who believed that there would be a fulfillment of what was spoken to her by the Lord" (v. 45). This second "blessed" is a different Greek word than the first. This is the same word Jesus uses in the Beatitudes: "Blessed are the poor in spirit" (Matthew 5:3). This second word for "blessed" is sometimes translated as "happy."

Despite the long journey, despite the physical discomfort and pain that comes with pregnancy and childbirth, despite the difficult conversations Mary will need to have in the coming months, despite the confusion and sheer weight of it all, despite what looks, from a worldly perspective, to be a terrible mess—there is deep joy.

Elizabeth does not create this joy, but in naming it she opens Mary up to it in a new way. Elizabeth does not, herself, bless Mary, but in reminding her of her blessed status, she allows Mary to more fully live into the life God offers.

I find this relationship between Elizabeth and Mary to be quite beautiful. I know there are times when I feel overwhelmed and want to run "with haste" to someone who will welcome me, understand me, and bless me. I hope there are times when I am that person whom others want to come to, and that I can offer deep compassion and blessing, just as Elizabeth does.

CONNECT:

If you are feeling vulnerable and overwhelmed right now, reach out to someone you trust who can offer a listening ear and a blessing. If you know of someone who is struggling, reach out to them and see if they would like a chance to visit.

CONSIDER:

What does it mean to speak words of blessing to others? What does it mean to receive words of blessing? When do you have an opportunity to give and receive blessings? What words of blessing do you think God wants you to hear right now?

December 22

MARY SINGS GOD'S JUSTICE

READ:
Luke 1:46–56

REFLECT:
These words from Mary are some of the most well known and well loved in the Christian Scriptures. For years I thought Mary spoke them in response to Gabriel's news that she would bear Jesus, but that's not the case. Mary's stirring words of holy rebellion are spoken by the weary teenager only *after* the words of blessing are spoken by her older, wiser, likely also exhausted and possibly nauseous relative Elizabeth. "Blessed are you among women," says Elizabeth, and *then* Mary proclaims: "My soul magnifies the Lord" and "all generations will call me blessed" (Luke 1:42, 46, 48).

It is worth paying attention to the verb tenses in this passage. Mary uses present tense for what she is doing: magnifying God. She uses future tense for what all generations will do: call her blessed. But she uses past tense for what God has done: shown strength with his arm, scattered the proud, brought down the powerful, lifted up the lowly, filled the hungry, sent the rich away empty.

For first-century Jewish people living under Roman imperial rule, it surely didn't seem like the powerful had been brought down or the hungry had been filled. It's a curious choice on Mary's part. But I think it speaks to the second blessing that Elizabeth bestows on her: "Blessed is she who believed that there would be a fulfillment of what was spoken to her by the Lord" (v. 45).

Mary's use of the past tense is an indication that she *does* believe there will be a fulfillment of what was spoken to her—actually, she believes that *there is already* a fulfillment of the promise.

Elizabeth's words send us back to the words of Gabriel, to see what, exactly, was spoken to Mary: "The Lord God will give to [your child] the throne of his ancestor David. He will reign over the house of Jacob forever, and of his kingdom there will be no end. . . . The child to be born will be holy; he will be called Son of God" (vv. 32–33, 35). Mary certainly has some reason to believe the words of Gabriel. She, a virgin, is pregnant, as is her older (too old) relative Elizabeth. Still, it feels overwhelming to take in all this promise— that the child will be holy and will reign over the house of Jacob.

Notice, too, that Mary goes beyond even what "was spoken to her by the Lord"—or at least beyond what we heard spoken to her. She believes the promise *and* she understands what the promise will mean for the world. With this deep understanding of Gabriel's words, Mary sings of the revolutionary scope of God's promise being realized through the incarnation: the powerful will be cast down and the lowly lifted up; the hungry will be fed and the rich sent away empty. As she bears Jesus in her body, she lives the fact of God's past-tense activity (Jesus' conception) that signals an already-here but not-yet-fully-realized liberation.

When we speak of God, sing of God, think of God, I fear we often limit our verb tenses. We speak of the past: when we were saved, when we were baptized, when God did that miraculous thing in our life, when we had a powerful spiritual experience. Or we speak of the present: where we are now, our current faith community, the glimpses God is allowing in the midst of our daily lives. Or we look to the future: the fulfillment of God's promises to bring peace and justice to earth, to wipe every tear from our eyes.

One of the deep gifts of Mary's song is that it holds all time together in the sacred space of the incarnation. It reminds us that the Mighty One, embodied in Jesus, is our beginning and our end, the Alpha and Omega, the one who was and is and is to come. In these days of Advent, as we prepare for the coming of the Christ child, may our hearts, like Mary's, magnify our God!

CONNECT:

There are many musical settings for this scripture passage, often called the Magnificat. Find a setting that you like (on a CD or a video or audio streaming service) and pause to listen to it several times throughout your day. (Some examples you could search for: "My Soul Cries Out [Canticle of the Turning]" by Rory Cooney; "With Mary Sing Magnificat" by Jeannette Lindholm; "My Soul Proclaims with Wonder" by Carl Daw Jr.; "Magnificat" by J. S. Bach; "The Annunciation and Magnificat" from *Holden Evening Prayer* by Marty Haugen; "Magnificat" by Christine Donkin.)

CONSIDER:

In your context, what would it look like for the powerful to be brought down from their thrones? For the lowly to be lifted up? Who are the hungry around you that need to be filled? Is there an action you can take this week to live out Mary's song?

December 23

MARY GIVES BIRTH

READ:
Luke 2:1–7

REFLECT:
We took a family trip to Walt Disney World when I was pregnant with my youngest, and I ended up doing a whole lot of waiting around for others to finish their rides. It seemed like every attraction, even the most mild and harmless, had this frustrating line on its bold WARNING sign: "Expectant mothers should not ride." I was most disappointed to miss the safari ride; apparently bumping along a paved road in a jeep posed too great a risk to my pregnancy.

And yet here is Mary, nearly nine months pregnant, traveling seventy-plus miles over rough terrain. We don't know exactly how she traveled, but it was likely by foot or donkey. Nothing as luxurious as a jeep.

Obviously, this census came at a very bad time for Mary and Joseph, but Emperor Augustus didn't really care. So off went the engaged couple to Bethlehem. Theories abound about why this journey happened—from scholars who argue the entire trip is a literary construct to comply with earlier messianic prophecies to those who explain how registering in Bethlehem allowed Joseph to exploit an ancient tax loophole.

In any case, whether it is because of her emperor, her narrator, or her finance-conscious fiancé, Mary is compelled by those with power to make a very inconvenient, and no doubt uncomfortable, journey.

In the last few weeks of pregnancy, almost all mothers-to-be are exhausted, with a sore back and quite possibly swollen ankles. This could not have been an easy journey for Mary, but she really doesn't have a choice.

And once she is finally in Bethlehem, wouldn't you know it, there's "no room at the inn." It's quite possible that the "inn" referenced here is not like a hotel, but rather a guest room in a family member's home. Mary and Joseph may not be traveling around, knocking on strangers' doors, but simply crashing on the couch in a relative's house because the guestroom is already taken. They likely slept in the main family room of the home, where people would often bring their animals in overnight—which would account for the presence of a feeding trough that doubles as a bassinet.

We can't be sure of the circumstances of Jesus' birth, because the writer of Luke really doesn't give us much detail. Most of what we include in our nativity scenes and Christmas pageants comes from human imagination rather than biblical explanation. But we do know that the circumstances under which Mary gives birth are less than ideal. She is away from home, with no private space—and probably no bed—in which to have this child. Even in the best of circumstances, childbirth is painful—and not a little terrifying. It is difficult to imagine the intensity of emotion Mary experiences as she pushes her baby out of her body and into the world.

We can imagine a lot of activity going on around Mary as she gives birth: chattering relatives, bleating sheep, lowing cattle, noisy neighbors. But in this precious, holy moment, the focus narrows onto this young woman and the vulnerable life she has brought into the world: "And she gave birth to her firstborn son and wrapped him in bands of cloth, and laid him in a manger" (Luke 2:7).

We know the journey has been hard. We know the labor was grueling. We know the world will be cruel. But right now, there is the holy joy of new life; there is the tender care of a young mother; there is all the wonder and promise of God lying there, right in front of us.

CONNECT:

Look at baby pictures of yourself or others you love. If you have given birth or witnessed someone else give birth, think about that experience. Ask someone to tell you about their experience giving birth.

CONSIDER:

Think about times in your life when all the distractions seemed to fade away and you focused in on just one thing. Are there big events where this happened for you? Are there smaller activities that help bring you more deeply into the moment? How can you more fully attend to the wonder of each moment?

MARY TREASURES
AND PONDERS

READ:
Luke 2:8–20

REFLECT:
This story of Jesus' birth has a warm glow around it as we remember Christmas Eve services filled with candlelight and familiar hymns. When we hear these words, we envision the nativity scene: a loyal father and loving mother gazing down contentedly at their blissfully peaceful newborn son. By all means, we should hold that warmth in our hearts and enjoy the joyful memories. And we should also acknowledge that the holy family was quite possibly not in such a serene state at this point in the story.

After a long and difficult journey, Mary gives birth in a strange town, in a strange room, with an animal feeding trough for her son's bed. None of this was in her birth plan. There is, for some new mothers, a surge of joy at holding their child for the first time, looking into the face of the one who has been hidden within their body for the past months. And mixed with the joy they may feel, there is also exhaustion, deep weariness, and fear—a terrifying realization of how vulnerable this human is that they love so deeply.

Amid all this, Mary receives unexpected visitors: the shepherds. They have come straight from the fields "with haste," so they are likely dirty, smelly, out of breath. Imagine Mary's surprise when this crew bursts in to gape at the child in the manger, when they start telling anyone who will listen about the angel, the good news, the multitude of heavenly host. It must have been disconcerting, to say the least. But Mary does not kick them out; she does not ask what they are doing there. She does not start yelling or break down in tears. She "treasured all these words and pondered them in her heart" (Luke 2:19).

This is the second time we are told that Mary *pondered*. It is a lovely word. *Pondering* suggests a calm center, a certain interior spaciousness, an ability to step back to a place of perspective and contemplation—which is not the state I imagine *I* would be in if the angel Gabriel visited me (Luke 1:29), or if a group of rough strangers crashed into my space right after I gave birth and started telling stories of more angel visitations.

I can imagine myself doing many things if I were in a situation similar to Mary's. I might run or hide, cry or yell, start nervously fidgeting or be completely unable to move at all. What I struggle to imagine is that I would be able to *ponder* this angel presence, the unbelievable message from the excitable shepherds—to take the significance of these holy moments into my being and hold them tenderly, with curiosity, gratitude, and wonder.

As hard as birthing Jesus was, mothering him surely proved much more difficult. And isn't that the way it always is? Whether we are bringing life to a new human, to a new community, to an artistic work, to a project, or to an idea, the initial creation is often difficult, but it is also exciting. Creative work is carried forward by longing, anticipation, and holy energy. Then comes the equally important but less recognized work of nurturing and sustaining our creations.

Mary does not just give birth to Jesus; she raises him. She cares for him, nurtures him, teaches him, walks with him all through his life. And I wonder whether all this pondering at the beginning of her journey is part of what helped her with the ongoing challenges of motherhood. She maintained the energy of creation; she noticed the presence and work of God; she sat at the still center of the miracle that was her life and held it as a treasure.

May we do the same in these holy days of Christmas.

CONNECT:

Center yourself in God's presence. With God, walk through what you expect of your day tomorrow and choose a time—even just ten minutes—when you will step away from the holiday activities to read the Christmas blessing in this book, meditate on the artwork, and *ponder* God's immeasurable love for you. Put this time on your calendar or write it on a paper you will see.

CONSIDER:

What have you created? How would you compare the difficulty of creating to the difficulty of nurturing what you created? Where did you get energy for the creative part of your work? Where did you find energy to sustain your creation? Where is God present for you in the process of creation and the task of sustaining?

CHRISTMAS BLESSING
FROM MARY

Dear one, I wish you had been there:
 to see the startling light, to hear Gabriel's brazen promise;
 to journey into the hill country, to receive Elizabeth's bold blessing;
 to look with the Spirit's eye,
 to sing of joy and justice that echoes through the ages.

Oh how I wish you had been there:
 with sore feet, aching back, Joseph's encouraging words,
 and Bethlehem on the horizon;
 with, finally, a place to rest,
 then the pain (the pain!) and the pushing,
 and the baby—my baby—bloody and perfect in the manger.

I would love for you to have been there,
 gathered with the shepherds
 who had somehow found their odd sign
 in this scene of me and Joseph and my swaddled child.

But you were not there, then.
You are here, now.
I cannot offer you the baby to hold and rock and smell.
So I offer you these words to wrap tenderly in cloth,
 and to lay in the manger of your heart:

In all that God calls you to do and to be,
    may you have courage
    to say yes to the mystery.

In times of excitement, grief, joy, and fear,
    may you have loved ones
    to offer companionship and blessing.

In the labor of creation,
    may you be strong,
    may you be flexible,
    may you know joy.

May you, beloved child,
    ponder deeply each divine message you hear,
    whether from angel or shepherd.
May you ponder and treasure
    every gift you receive
    from the holy hand of God.

December 26

MARY PRESENTS
JESUS AT THE TEMPLE

READ:
Luke 2:21–35

REFLECT:
While many things about Mary's story are extraordinary, in today's reading she does exactly what one would expect a first-century Jewish mother to do: she has her son circumcised and makes the journey to the temple in Jerusalem to present her firstborn child and purify herself after childbirth. She is faithful to the rituals of her religious community, even as her experience with God goes so far beyond the confines of those rituals.

Surely some people—most notably Joseph—supported Mary through her unusual pregnancy, but she likely had to deal with sideways looks and outright insults from those around her. In the Qur'an, which also offers an account of this story, when Mary carries her newborn baby into town, the people say that she is evil, at which point the infant Jesus begins speaking and explains to them that he is a prophet (Qur'an 19:27–33). In the biblical account, we are not specifically told about how the community treats Mary, but I imagine the Qur'an is accurate in portraying the hostility of many townspeople.

Fortunately, Mary does not equate the actions of God's people with the actions of God. She does not use the misguided comments of other Jewish people as a reason to abandon her faith or an excuse to neglect the actions that are part of her religious observance. Mary continues on, not just in her personal relationship with God—which is arguably the most intimate and intense relationship any human has ever had with God—but also with her participation in the faith community.

In Luke 4, as an introduction to Jesus' first sermon, we read that Jesus "went to the synagogue on the sabbath day, as was his custom" (v. 16). *As was his custom.* Mary's faithful participation in the life of her religious community is an important foundation for Jesus' own life of faith. Her personal relationship with God is a beautiful thing, but it is her outward participation in the community that others, including her son, can witness and emulate.

When we participate in a faith community, we come into contact with other people of faith—which, granted, is sometimes a pain. It is also true, though, that other people have wisdom and insight that can help us on our own faith journey. If Mary had not taken Jesus to the temple, she would not have encountered Simeon and would not have heard his confirmation of her son's identity: "My eyes have seen your salvation" (Luke 2:30).

It must have been a relief for Mary to hear these words firsthand from a flesh-and-blood human person. And to have Joseph there to also witness the promise and confirm the message. Simeon's statement would have been a reassurance that she hadn't just imagined Gabriel's visit, that the shepherds hadn't been making up a story for their own amusement. What a blessed relief to know that other people saw in her son exactly what Gabriel had promised.

Simeon's words are certainly a blessing to her, though his final words are a pretty odd sort of blessing: "A sword will pierce your own soul too" (v. 35). These are not the words any mother wants to hear. Yet somehow, they are part of Simeon's blessing.

I suppose it is the blessing of truth—a mixed blessing to be sure. As difficult as these words must have been for Mary to hear, I wonder whether she thought back to them through the years, pulled them out and wrapped them around her when things got difficult—when she didn't understand her son, when she was so terribly afraid of what they would do to him. Does knowing a sword will pierce your soul make it any easier when the blow actually comes?

These are the complexities we face when we participate in a faith community, when we seek relationships with others in our connections with God. The "just me and God" mentality can be awfully tempting, but Mary demonstrates faithfulness to and in and through a religious community. That is the type of faith that Jesus was taught and that he lived out in his ministry.

Sometimes, faith in community is more difficult than faith on our own. But it is in community that we will find the true blessing.

CONNECT:

In addition to worshiping with your own church this week (if you have one), try to visit—in person or online—another faith community as well. Speak with someone there about how that community supports their faith.

CONSIDER:

What religious rituals are most meaningful for you? Why? What gifts have you received from your faith community? What gifts do you offer? Do you carry any pain or shame from harmful faith communities? If you are not currently part of a faith community, think about what type of community could support you in your faith. If you are currently part of a faith community that does not feel like a healthy, nurturing space, what would it mean to find a new faith community?

December 27

MARY WELCOMES THE MAGI

READ:
Matthew 2:1–12

REFLECT:
It's no wonder this story of the magi echoes through the centuries in stories and poems, paintings, and music. It has so many dramatic elements: the fascinating foreigners, the manipulative king, the treacherous journey, the mysterious star, the expensive (and somewhat odd) gifts. Often overlooked, at the center of all the drama, is Mary. While the wise men are observing the night sky, traveling through the desert, talking to King Herod, and searching for the child, Mary is in Bethlehem, caring for her son. She is changing his swaddling clothes, and then his regular clothes; nursing him, then slowly introducing solid food; picking up the stray nails left on the floor by her carpenter husband so that Jesus doesn't try to eat them.

While the wise men are fixated on finding Jesus, Mary is not waiting for them. She is living her life. What was it like for her that day the wise men showed up? Had she noticed the strange star in the sky? Did she sense that something was going to happen?

I wonder whether the arrival of the wise men felt like an interruption or an affirmation for Mary. Did she recognize the royal significance of the gifts they brought? Did she appreciate the gold, frankincense, and myrrh? Or did she sell them to buy more swaddling clothes? Because really, what is a toddler going to do with frankincense?

Clearly these foreigners considered Jesus to be a special child. This, of course, was not a new concept for Mary. Gabriel had told her that her child would "reign over the house of Jacob forever" (Luke 1:33). Elizabeth had called Mary's child her "Lord" (v. 43). Since the shepherds "made known what had been told them about this child" (Luke 2:17), they surely reported that the angels had said he was the Messiah. And Simeon referred to Jesus as God's "salvation" (v. 30).

But I wonder whether a little chill went through her when the wise men referred to him as "king of the Jews." I wonder whether she felt a tight ball of fear in her stomach when the visitors mentioned that they had stopped by Herod's palace for a little chat on their way to see Jesus. Surely Mary knew—surely everyone not from a foreign country knew—how Herod would respond to the merest suggestion that anyone besides him was king of anything. "Oh no," she must have thought, "I hope these guys didn't tell Herod they were looking for a newborn king!"

Of course, they had told Herod exactly that. And the thought of Herod knowing about her child must have terrified Mary. I know the text says that the wise men were warned in a dream not to return to Herod. And God does, certainly, speak through dreams. I don't want to discount the power of God at work in this story in any way.

Still, I wonder whether their dreams were aided a bit by Mary. Surely she wasn't in a position to instruct these powerful, rich foreigners about where they could go and whom they could talk to. But maybe she dropped hints. "You know, if you take a *different* route home, you could stop by this fabulous little restaurant . . ." "Sometimes that Herod guy is not the most fun to talk to . . ." Or maybe she even whispered to them as they slept: "Please, please don't tell Herod about my son. Please take a different route home."

This visit from the wise men reminds Mary of all that is completely out of her control. And this story can remind us of the same thing. We cannot control the blessings that drop in unexpected. We cannot control the threats that lurk in the shadows. We can love and care for those God gives us to love and care for to the best of our ability, but we can't control how other people treat them—for good or for ill.

In this reminder of how little control we often have, we are also reminded that God is at work—through creation, through our dreams, through basic common sense. For all that we cannot control, we can rest in the power of God.

CONNECT:

Get three pieces of paper to represent the gold, frankincense, and myrrh that the magi brought to baby Jesus. (You can be as artistic with this as you want. Or not.) On each piece of paper, write a passage from the Bible that reminds you of God's loving power (a few suggestions: Joshua 2:11; Psalms 21:13; 63:2; 130:7; 147:5; Luke 1:35, 37, 51).

CONSIDER:

When have you received an unexpected blessing—maybe a surprise gift or visit from a friend? When have you felt fear sneak up on you? What helps you rest in God's steady power when things feel out of control?

MARY ESCAPES TO EGYPT

READ:
Matthew 2:13–15, 19–23

REFLECT:
This is the second time an angel has shown up in Joseph's dreams. The first time, the angel told Joseph to marry Mary even though she was pregnant—that her child was from the Holy Spirit (Matthew 1:20). This time, the angel tells Joseph to take his family to Egypt because Herod wants to destroy Mary's child.

I imagine this was a rather awkward conversation between Joseph and Mary as he tried to explain to her that they needed to uproot their entire life and move to another country because the king wanted to kill their baby. Moving to a foreign country with a toddler is something a mother might be hesitant to do, but Mary has a couple of reasons to go along with Joseph's plan.

First, she knows that this dream angel is more than a figment of Joseph's overactive dream imagination. The angel gave Joseph good and true counsel the first time around. Mary's baby really was of the Holy Spirit, and Joseph's staying with Mary kept her secure and safe in what could have been a dangerous situation.

Second, Mary knows enough about who her son is to understand the threat he might pose to Herod. Yes, Jesus is just a toddler at this point, but Mary has heard the powerful prophecies about him. And she likely knows how fragile Herod's ego is. After the strange visitors from the east, Mary can see what might be coming and may have welcomed Joseph's suggestion to leave town.

Yet even if Mary understands the necessity of leaving Bethlehem, how terrifying it must have been to abandon her home by night and travel with her young child into a foreign country. The journey was surely difficult, and I imagine there were many struggles as she worked to raise her child in Egypt. Whom did she ask for advice when he was sick or misbehaving? Whom could she ask to watch him for an afternoon when she desperately needed a nap? Whom did Jesus have playdates with? It can be difficult to find community in a foreign land.

And how did she feel when Joseph told her that the angel said it was time to go back home? I suppose Mary had learned to listen when Joseph said, "An angel came to me in a dream last night." Still, there must have been some trepidation about returning to the place where the king had wanted her child killed.

At the beginning of Jesus' life, Mary is doing the always difficult work of mothering in particularly difficult circumstances. She bears the logistical and emotional strain of moving away from home. She carries a deep fear for her child, knowing that very powerful people want to kill him. She helps Joseph with the physical labor of packing and endures the grueling travel—first to Egypt, then to Nazareth.

You may also have experienced a time when your life just seemed to get more and more difficult, more and more stressful; a time when you felt completely overwhelmed. Such challenges feel impossible. And yet when we really have to do something, we often . . . just . . . do it.

Do you have those moments in your life that you look back on and wonder how you ever made it through? A difficult move. A particularly heavy work or school load. A serious illness experienced by you or a loved one. A daunting project. A series of crises.

I imagine Mary looked back on these early years of Jesus' life like that. The physical and emotional stress of these moves was immense. The fear for her son's life must have been nearly unbearable. Being a new mother in a new community without family and friends around would have been so hard.

But we know how it goes. You do what you have to do. (It's nice, of course, to have angel confirmation.) Sometimes, in the midst of it all, we are too busy getting through to even see God's presence with us. But when we look back, we know that what we did was incredible, and that the hand of God was with us, guiding us through.

CONNECT:

As you think about the journeys that Mary took, I commend to you the spiritual practice of using a labyrinth. Labyrinths provide an opportunity to prayerfully consider your own journey with God through life. (To find a labyrinth to walk, see the website World-Wide Labyrinth Locator. You can also print a finger labyrinth [images available online] or search an online video site for "walking a labyrinth.")

CONSIDER:

Think back to a difficult, stressful period in your own life. How did you make it through? Looking back, how do you believe God supported you in that work? How can you offer support to someone you know who is going through a difficult time?

December 29

MARY LOSES JESUS

READ:
Luke 2:41–52

REFLECT:
I love that it takes Mary a full day to realize Jesus isn't with them. It tells me that she is not a "helicopter mom." She has other things to do besides fret over Jesus all the time. She has other children to tend to, friends to talk with, maybe more things to ponder in her heart as they head home after a meaningful Passover celebration. It tells me that she trusts her son and her community. She simply assumes Jesus is nearby, walking with a family member or friend.

Toward the end of the day, though, she and Joseph start to look for Jesus. It's time to gather the family together—to have all the kids put on their jammies, brush their teeth, and hear a bedtime story. Only, Jesus is nowhere to be found.

"A sword will pierce your own soul too" (Luke 2:35). I wonder how many times these words from Simeon echoed in Mary's heart as she went from group to group trying to find Jesus. But he was nowhere to be found. Despite having just walked for a full day, Mary and Joseph turn around and walk all the way back to Jerusalem.

For us, as readers, the anxiety is resolved in six words: "After three days they found him" (v. 46). For Mary, though, it is not six words, it is *three days*. Mary and Joseph finally find Jesus in the temple, talking to the teachers. Then here, in the temple, in front of these (male) teachers, it is Mary, not Joseph, who speaks to Jesus:

"Child, why have you treated us like this? Look, your father and I have been searching for you in great anxiety" (v. 48).

When we read this story, we usually focus on how wise Jesus is at such a young age, how this story points to the great religious teacher that Jesus will soon become. But regardless of how deep his understanding of Torah is, how theologically brilliant his religious discourse is, his mother is not wrong to scold him for his treatment of his parents. The past four days have been agonizing for Mary and Joseph. Who knows how many ways Mary had envisioned her son to be maimed or ill or dead as she looked for him all over Jerusalem. Jesus may have a deep understanding of religious texts and law, but he still has things to learn from his mother about caring for others.

We generally read Jesus' question here as criticism: "Why were you searching for me? Did you not know that I must be in my Father's house?" (v. 49). And maybe it is. Or maybe it is an actual question. Maybe Jesus is honestly confused and didn't realize that his parents would be worried, that they would spend three agonizing days looking for him. Maybe, like most twelve-year-olds, Jesus doesn't yet realize that he is not the center of the universe. (And maybe, for the almighty God who actually *is* the center of the universe, this is a particularly hard lesson of the incarnation.) It seems that Jesus did learn from this event; we are told that he went home with his parents "and was obedient to them" (v. 51).

I'll grant that Mary and Jesus present a unique situation, but the reality is that all relationships are layered and complicated. Each person we interact with has something to teach us and something to learn from us. We can learn from others by watching what they do and paying attention to how they live out their faith. We can learn from others by listening to their words and to the emotions behind those words. We can also learn by recognizing how our actions affect those around us.

And we can teach others—even when we don't realize it. We teach others when we prioritize faith commitments, when we relax with a group of friends and don't fret and worry about every detail, when we share our sincere emotions. As teachers and as learners, we can grow together in faithfulness.

CONNECT:

Do an online image search for "Mary finds Jesus in the temple" and choose one image to contemplate. What do you notice about the image? How would you describe Jesus here? How would you describe Mary? What new insights or questions about the story does this image bring up in your mind?

CONSIDER:

Who have been the most important teachers in your life—whether or not they were people labeled "teachers"? What is an important lesson you have learned? Do you learn more from listening to people or from watching them? What is one thing you would like people to learn from you? How can you communicate this lesson through your words and actions?

December 30

MARY GOES TO A PARTY

READ:
John 2:1–12

REFLECT:
In the gospel of John, Jesus' mother is never named nor is the birth story of Jesus told. The gospel begins with an adult Jesus, yet Mary still plays an important role. The first sign that Jesus performs in John gives us insight into the significance of the relationship between Jesus and his mother.

Both Jesus and Mary are at a wedding party in Cana when Mary notices that the wine is gone. It seems that Mary is aware of the situation before most of the other guests—possibly even before the steward. Maybe she was close to the bride who confided in her about the disastrous situation. Maybe she was just particularly observant; tending to children can definitely heighten one's ability to assess a situation quickly and see problems emerging before they explode into crises.

I think it says something about Mary that she notices the wine has run out. And perhaps it says even more about her that she cares. She knows the shame it could bring on the new bride and groom if they were to run out of wine at their wedding. She sees the wedding guests—her friends and family—having fun around her and does not want anything to disrupt the festivities. Mary both notices *and* cares.

And so she tells her son—who also happens to be God's Son— "They have no wine" (John 2:3). In this one line, we get a glimpse into this complicated mother-son relationship; we gain insight into Mary's view of Jesus. In John's gospel, this is Jesus' first sign; it causes his disciples to believe in him. But Mary already understands something about Jesus' identity and power. Looking at the other gospels, we can gather clues about how Mary knows Jesus can work miracles. But here in John, it is a mystery. There is simply *something* there between mother and son, some deep knowledge Mary has of her firstborn that leads her to tell him: "They have no wine."

In this exchange between Jesus and his mother, he comes off as a bit of the pouty teenager: "That's not my problem. Leave me alone. I'm trying to party with my friends here." (Of course, I'm paraphrasing.) And Mary, like any wise mother, doesn't engage with his protests; she simply says to the servants, "Do whatever he tells you" (v. 5).

Those are the last words Mary speaks in this story. These are actually the last words Mary speaks in the entire gospel of John. She doesn't seem to worry about the wine situation after that. She knows Jesus will take care of it—and he does. Sometimes that is one of the most difficult parts of being a parent, a teacher, a person who seeks to nurture others—pointing someone in what you hope is the right direction and then walking away, letting them take care of things in their own way and their own time.

While Luke, Matthew, and John all share different stories about the mother of Jesus, all three gospels reveal Mary to be a woman of deep faithfulness and wisdom. The two lines Mary speaks in the gospel of John reveal characteristics I would like to develop in my own life.

"They have no wine." "Do whatever he tells you." In these few words, we see that Mary is attentive and compassionate. She is a practical problem-solver and an astute delegator. She is a mother who loves and challenges her child. She is a faithful woman who believes in the power and presence of God. May we live into such wisdom and faithfulness as we prepare to begin a new year.

CONNECT:

Think back through the stories we have read about Mary. Make a list of all the characteristics you see in the mother of Jesus. Circle two or three of these characteristics that you would like to further develop in yourself. Pray for the guidance and support of the Holy Spirit as you grow in faithfulness.

CONSIDER:

Why do you think Mary had so much trust in Jesus? What do you feel is your level of trust in Jesus right now? What diminishes your trust? What helps your trust grow?

MARY'S BLESSING

My fellow travelers—
   you who flee danger,
   and you who return home;
   you who make a faithful pilgrimage,
   and you who search for what is lost:

I cannot tell where the road will lead,
   who will accompany you,
   or what stars might guide you.

I cannot promise ease or safety.
I cannot say whether you will have to turn around
   to go back for something left behind.
I cannot guarantee that every blessing you receive on the way
   will be a blessing you want.

But I hope *this* blessing is one you will carry,
   a blessing to ride comfortably in your pocket,
   or rest softly in your hands;
   a blessing to accompany you, whatever the journey brings:

May you know God in your own heart
   and in the heart of your faith community.
May you be brave toward your fear
   and persistent through deep difficulties.

May you hold your responsibilities faithfully
    and lightly—with grace and joy.
May you teach well
    and learn well.
May you give attention and compassion
    to the lives that surround you,
        and to your own hard and beautiful life.

ANNA, THE WEEPING MOTHERS, AND WISDOM

January 1

ANNA PRAISES GOD

READ:
Luke 2:36–38

REFLECT:
These verses conclude the story of Jesus' dedication in the temple that we began on December 26. This story tells of two elderly people at the temple who speak about the Christ child. I do not intend to diminish Simeon, who is obviously, as the text tells us, righteous and devout. He is a faithful man who is attuned enough to the Holy Spirit to be led to the temple on the day Jesus shows up. Still, while Simeon is identified as a "man," Anna is introduced as a "prophet" (Luke 2:25, 36). An authority is given to Anna beyond what Simeon holds. Only three living people are named as prophets in the Gospels: John the Baptist, Jesus, and Anna.

While Simeon "came into the temple," Anna "never left the temple" (vv. 27, 37). She "worshiped there with fasting and prayer night and day." Of course, simply being in the temple—even being there "night and day"—does not make one righteous. In the Gospels, the temple is a conflicted space. It is where Jesus teaches as well as where religious leaders plot against Jesus (for example, see Luke 19:47). The temple is the setting for the parable about the Pharisee and the tax collector who both come to pray, but only the humble tax collector "went down to his home justified" (Luke 18:14). And of course we have the (in)famous scene of Jesus turning over the tables in the temple court (Luke 19:45–48).

To be sure, there are plenty of unpleasant people who spend a lot of time at church yet still act in ungodly, harmful ways; plenty of people who cultivate a religious veneer for their own selfish purposes. Being in a religious building and doing "churchy" things is obviously no guarantee of a righteous life. But for some, like Anna, their presence with the religious community is sincere, their prayer is a true connection to the divine, and the spiritual disciplines they practice are for God and for themselves rather than for the appearance of it all. Anna inhabits the sacred space of the temple not for show, not to gain prestige, not even because it's what she is *supposed* to do; she inhabits the temple as a means of being in relationship with God and with God's people.

We are told that Anna approaches the holy family in the temple "at that moment" (Luke 2:38). Which, of course, means we have to look back and see what exactly "that moment" was: when Simeon tells Mary, "A sword will pierce your own soul too" (v. 35). *That* moment. It must have been a painful moment for Mary. Confusing. Heartbreaking. Frightening. Simeon's words are true but heavy. Anna comes right at *that moment* and begins to praise God. Even though we do not hear the specific words that Anna speaks, we can imagine what a gift these words of praise must be for Mary *at that moment*.

While the grief and fear—the piercing swords—that Simeon speaks of are real, Anna affirms that the bigger, the more immanent and eternal reality, is the redemption God is bringing to the world in Jesus. Many scholars will point out that the gospel of Luke frequently pairs male and female characters together in the narrative and in parables. (Consider the annunciations to Zechariah and Mary in Luke 1; the parables of the woman who lost her coin and the man who lost his son in Luke 15.) But Anna shows up here to provide not just gender balance, but theological balance. Yes, the reality of Jesus' life—and therefore the lives of his parents—will be difficult and painful. *And* the reality of God's life participating in the world through Jesus is worthy of praise and celebration. The crucifixion is real. The resurrection is also real—and more powerful.

While true prophets might speak hard truths, they also radiate hope and joy; they believe deeply in redemption because they are deeply connected to the Redeemer. It is because of Anna's constant presence at the temple, because of her prayer and fasting, that she is able to be present for the holy family *at that moment*, to offer praise and hope.

CONNECT:
Use your holy imagination to write down the words Anna might have spoken to Mary *at that moment* in the temple.

CONSIDER:
What hard truths about your own life do you need to accept? What swords are piercing your soul? And what words of life and hope does God have for you *at this moment*? What might the prophet Anna say to you?

ANNA'S BLESSING

I hold the grief of my widowhood
    lightly and tenderly within myself.
It is a sorrow and also a joy.
It is part of me.
It is what it is.

I wear the mantle of prophet
    carefully and with trepidation.
It is a burden and also a privilege.
It is part of me.
It is what it is.

My life is worship and prayer,
    not always on my knees,
    not always looking toward heaven,
    but always connecting
    somehow
    to God who,
    somehow,
    wants to abide with me.

Through my grief, with my prophetic power,
    in the temple that is wherever you are now,
I pray this blessing with hands outstretched:

May your worship bring joy.
May your fasting bring clarity.
May your prayers be powerful.
May your praise ease the world's fear.
May your words be true.
May you be named and respected
    in the roles that God has given you.

January 3

THE MOTHERS WEEP

READ:
Matthew 2:16–18

REFLECT:
This is not the first time in Scripture we have seen a powerful ruler demand the murder of male children. All the way back in Exodus, Pharaoh feared the growing number of Hebrews and instructed his people to throw all the male Hebrew babies into the Nile River (Exodus 1:22). The text quoted in today's scripture reading is Jeremiah 31:15, which is set in the midst of the Babylonian exile. These children "that are no more" have been forcibly removed from their homes; the lamenting mothers have no idea whether their children are alive or dead.

These ancient mothers are kin to the Mothers of the Plaza de Mayo in Argentina who mourned their "disappeared" children and demanded that the dictator return their children to them alive. They are kin to the Central American mothers riding a bus through Mexico today, searching for their children who have fled home because of violence and economic hardships.

These ancient mothers are kin to enslaved African mothers whose children were ripped from their arms and sold to strangers. They are kin to Indigenous mothers whose children were taken from them and sent to white schools, where many of them were abused and even killed. They are kin to Black and Indigenous mothers in the United States today, whose infants face unconscionable mortality rates, whose young adult children—particularly their sons—are too often imprisoned unjustly.

In reading of the wailing mothers in Bethlehem, I think of all the mothers throughout the centuries who have joined Rachel's weeping and lamentation as their children have been threatened and killed because of the pride, anger, greed, and fear of those with power.

While Jesus survives Herod's death threats, he is not unaffected. His family is forced to flee their home, and he spends formative years of his childhood in a foreign land. Surely the tears of his mother mingle with the tears of those weeping for their children in Bethlehem and across the centuries.

Jesus himself enters the role of grieving mother when he laments over Jerusalem and asks, "How often have I desired to gather your children together as a hen gathers her brood under her wings?" (Luke 13:34). Later, as his crucifixion nears, he approaches the city of Jerusalem and weeps over it, lamenting the injustices its people inflict on others and the injustices they suffer themselves (Luke 19:41).

With their tears of anguish, all these weeping mothers across the centuries reveal the depth and power of their love. It is a love that carries children into exile and back again; it is a love that risks all to move threatened children to freedom and safety; it is a love that speaks up against individuals and systems that oppress their children.

This mothering love, carried by people of all genders and rooted in the essence of God, is a power beyond that of Pharaoh or Herod. It is a power that cares for the vulnerable and threatens unjust systems. This mothering love is a power that gathers us under the divine wings and holds us, and all our beloveds, close to the heart of God.

CONNECT:
Think about who has wept for you over the years. Who has shown you a deep mothering love? Write a note of gratitude to one of these

mothering figures, or maybe a poem about your experience of their love. If they are living, consider sending them what you wrote.

CONSIDER:

How are children suffering in your community and in the broader world today? What suffering causes your heart to wail? What injustice do you most lament? Is God calling you to take any action—large or small—to care for these children and address the systems that cause their suffering?

January 4

BLESSING OF THE WEEPING MOTHERS

Dear child,
I weep for each spiritual wound you hold,
    for every physical harm you bear,
    for all that threatens your safety
    and diminishes the fullness of your life.
My tears flow from my love:
    love for the sweetness and the fierceness of your soul,
    love for the beauty of your strong and fragile body,
    love for that place of tender vulnerability
    you work so hard to protect.

I trust there are others to offer you
    blessings with laughter and light;
I hold out to you another blessing.
I hold out to you—
    with wailing and tears—
    a mother's blessing,
    birthed from deepest love:
In this precious and complicated life,
    may you know your worth, use your voice,
    welcome your tears, and find your people.
May you be fierce in the face of injustice
    and gentle, always, with yourself.

January 5

SOPHIA CHRIST IS PRESENT AT CREATION

READ:
John 1:1–5; Proverbs 8:22–36

REFLECT:
While the gospels of Matthew and Luke begin with the story of Jesus' birth, John's gospel begins with Christ's existence as *the Word* from the beginning of creation. The Greek term translated here as "Word" is *logos*, which is a masculine version of the Greek *sophia*—wisdom. When we read John 1 and Proverbs 8 together, we can see the parallels between the character of Wisdom in Proverbs and the Word in John. Both are intimately connected to God, both are integral to the creation of the world, and both bring life.

While the writer of John's gospel is, likely for his own cultural and theological reasons, careful to use the masculine term *logos* to identify Jesus, there is a clear connection between Jesus and the distinctly feminine *sophia* tradition. As followers of Jesus, we should attend not just to the strong women who surrounded him and those who are part of his family line, but also to the creative feminine energy that Jesus himself carries into the world as the Word/Wisdom of God.

Sophia Christ is an integral part of creation, present with God as every aspect of the world is brought into being, skillfully working with God to craft soil and plants, sky and ocean. She is a source of delight for others and One who experiences deep delight herself. She is an ultimate source of life and light for those who find her.

While the women we have journeyed with this Advent and Christmas season can be our companions in spirit and imagination, the resurrected Christ can accompany us in Spirit and truth. Jesus, whom we seek to follow every day and whom we especially celebrate in this holy season, is indeed Emmanuel, God-with-us. As God, Jesus moves between and beyond our constructed categories—including categories of space, time, and gender. Jesus is expansively present at creation; particularly present in first-century Judea, Samaria, and Galilee; and immanently present with each of us and all of us today.

The Holy One whom we worship is a powerful birthing Mother, a tender loving Father, a wise guiding Parent who exists in all space and time and beyond our gender constructs.

All of this may sound interesting (or confusing) from a theological perspective, but what does it mean for us in our day-to-day lives as disciples of Jesus? It means that whatever our current circumstances, we can have deep peace in knowing that the Holy One has been present since before creation, is present with us now, and will be present in the midst of whatever the future holds. It means that there is no part of our being that the divine One does not intimately understand; because God has become flesh, Jesus holds all genders. It means that we are lovingly accompanied by a creative power greater than the forces of destruction that we encounter in this world.

It means that every day, God delights in us and we are invited to delight in God.

CONNECT:
Throughout the day today, offer this simple breath prayer:
  Breathing in: God delights in me.
  Breathing out: I delight in God.

CONSIDER:

How do you respond to the idea of a feminine Christ? What do you think about it? How do you feel about it? Why do you think you have this response? How do your ideas about gender affect your relationship with God? How have the reflections you have read this Advent and Christmas season affected your understanding of gender, both in terms of how we relate to each other and in terms of how we relate to God?

SOPHIA'S BLESSING

My love,
    you are a delight—
    like watching springs bubble up
    and hills emerge;
    like feeling the first fertile soil
    and seeing tiny green sprouts;
    like gasping in wonder as stars fill the sky
    and ocean waves lap against immeasurable sand.
You are a delight and a joy, my love.

So the blessing I offer is a simple one:
Be who you are.
Be what you have been intended to be
    since the beginning of all things.
Be what I have created you to be:
    delightful
    delighted
    light
    life
    love.

GUIDES FOR GROUP USE

WORSHIP GUIDE

This worship material follows the scripture passages and themes of the *Expecting Emmanuel* devotionals. While people's worship experiences may be enriched by also using the daily devotions, these liturgies are designed to stand on their own and be meaningful even for those not engaging with the material more broadly.

Please note that the stories of the women in Jesus' genealogy contain substantial sexual content and elements of sexual violence. While the readings selected for worship do not delve too deeply into these aspects of the stories, church leaders should still be aware that discussing these women could bring up difficult feelings for people who have experienced sexualized violence. Please be prepared to provide resources and spiritual care for those who might have trauma responses to the material.

WORSHIP IMAGES

The images in this book from Michelle Burkholder are available for download at bit.ly/Expecting-Emmanuel.

CANDLE-LIGHTING

The candle themes suggested in the weekly liturgies are slightly different from the traditional themes. If you choose to use the suggested themes, you could easily keep the usual color pattern of three blue/purple candles and a pink candle to be lit on the third Sunday of Advent. You could also choose to have four candles of different colors to represent the four women we are highlighting.

The candle-lighting liturgies provided are designed to be used at the beginning of worship. If you will light the candles later in the service, you can pull out the litany to be used as a call to worship and then read the scripture passage and speak the candle-lighting words when the candles are lit.

CHILDREN'S TIME

Let's face it, friends, the stories of the women in Jesus' genealogy are not exactly G-rated. Rather than focus on the particular Bible stories during children's time, I suggest a more general focus on the idea of family trees.

For Advent 1: Talk to the children about family trees, and explain that the Bible tells us about some of the people who are part of Jesus' family tree. For some ideas of how to approach this, see the November 27 reflection. Be sensitive to issues of adoption and difficult family relationships as you talk with the children. You could ask the children whether they know the names of their grandparents and great-grandparents.

For Advent 2 through Epiphany: Invite a different person in the congregation to share each week about an ancestor whom they admire. Ask them to bring a picture (if possible), to tell a story about their ancestor, and to explain why they admire them.

PRAYER OF CONFESSION

(to be used any or every week)[1]

> Leader: God of shadows and light,
> our thoughts are not your thoughts.
> Our ways are not your ways.[2]
>
> All: *Hear our confession.*
> *Heal our hearts.*
> *Forgive our sins.*
>
> (*silence*)
>
> Leader: In Jesus you call us to hope
> All: *that your justice will prevail—*
> *that the hungry will be fed and the lowly lifted up.*
>
> Leader: In Jesus you call us to faith
> All: *in the mystery of your Presence in the world,*
> *and the truth that nothing will be impossible*
> *with you.*
>
> Leader: In Jesus you reveal your love,
> All: *that we might love more fully*
> *and know how deeply we are loved.*
>
> Leader: In Jesus you reveal your power—
> All: *a power with and for the vulnerable;*
> *a power held in mercy and grace.*

---

1. Note: This prayer of confession can be used in its entirety, or you can use just one of the stanzas between the two periods of silence. The first four stanzas correlate with the candles being lit during the four weeks of Advent; the final stanza corresponds to the Christ candle that is lit on Christmas 1, Christmas 2, and Epiphany.

2. Isaiah 55:8.

Leader: In Jesus you call us to joy—
All: *a joy that can hold the world's grief*
and its beauty.

(*silence*)

Leader: In the light of the Christ child,
in the shadow of the Most High,
we make our confession
and receive your forgiveness.
All: **Amen.**

OFFERTORY PRAYER (TO BE USED ANY OR EVERY WEEK)
Leader: Holy One, Emmanuel:
as you have given yourself to us
through the coming of the Christ child,
we also give ourselves to you.
All: *Receive these offerings,*
given in hope,[3]
that they may be part of your life
in this world.
Amen.

---

3. Note: The word "hope" in (line 6) can be replaced with the candle word for each week of Advent (hope, faith, love, power). For Christmas 1, Christmas 2, and Epiphany, replace "hope" with "joy."

Advent 1
TAMAR: ADVENT WAITING

Scripture reading: Genesis 38:1–27

Summarize Genesis 38:1–11: Tamar, the first woman listed in Jesus' genealogy, marries Judah's son Er. Er dies before he and Tamar have a child together, so Judah instructs his second son, Onan, to try to have a child with Tamar—as was the custom in that culture. Onan does not fulfill this duty to his brother, and he also dies. Judah has another son, Shelah, but Shelah is too young to marry Tamar; Judah is also afraid that Shelah will die like his brothers if he sleeps with Tamar.

Read Genesis 38:12–14.

Summarize Genesis 38:15–23: When Judah sees Tamar sitting at the city gate, he assumes she is a prostitute and he engages her services without recognizing who she is. He promises to send her a kid from his flock as payment, and she asks for his signet and cord and staff as a pledge until he sends the kid. But when Judah tries to send her the payment, nobody can find this mysterious prostitute, so he isn't able to retrieve his signet, cord, and staff.

Read Genesis 38:24–27.

SERMON SUGGESTIONS
Advent is often understood as a season of waiting, and in the two readings above, Tamar experiences two different types of waiting. The reflections for November 29 and 30 discuss how Tamar might have experienced these periods of waiting. The "Consider" questions for November 29 might be helpful in developing a sermon around this idea.

CANDLE-LIGHTING LITURGY

Scripture reading: Isaiah 40:27–31

Litany:

> Leader: Do you not know? Have you not heard?
>
> *All: The Holy One is the everlasting God,*
> *creator of heaven and earth.*
>
> Leader: God's energy flows through the world
> even when we are bone-tired,
>
> *All: God's power gives strength*
> *to the vulnerable and weak.*
>
> Leader: Do you not know? Have you not heard?
>
> *All: When we wait on the Holy One,*
> *God will renew our strength.*
>
> Leader: We shall run. We shall fly.
>
> *All: We shall walk boldly together*
> *toward the promises of God.*

Lighting the first Advent candle (hope):
As we light this candle of hope,
> we enter together into the holy season of Advent:
> a season of activity and of waiting,
> a season of shadow and of lights,
> a season of memory and of hope.

BENEDICTION OPTIONS

Based on worship theme:
May you know God's energy in your weariness, God's strength in your weakness, God's hope in your despair. In these days of Advent, may your waiting be blessed.

From "Tamar's Blessing" (December 1):
May the God of cloud and fire
    lead you in the wilderness,
    providing room for your grief,
    support for your anger,
    comfort for your pain,
    attention to each part of you.
May the God of cloud and fire
    burn away your shame
    to reveal your shining wisdom,
    your unmistakable power.

Advent 2

RAHAB: ON THE MARGINS

Scripture reading: Joshua 2:1–9, 12–15

SERMON SUGGESTIONS

Preaching on Rahab provides an opportunity to explore what it means to be on the margins and what can happen when we marginalize others. For further thoughts on this, see the reflections for December 2 and 3. The story of Rahab and the Christmas story of incarnation both remind us that power is sometimes held in unexpected ways.

CANDLE-LIGHTING LITURGY

Scripture reading: Hebrews 11:29–31

Litany:

Leader: By faith the people passed through the Red Sea.

All: By faith we come with open hearts.

Leader: By faith the walls of Jericho fell.

All: By faith we offer praise and prayers.

Leader: By faith Rahab received the spies in peace.

All: By faith we gather together for worship.

Lighting the second Advent candle (faith):

As we light this candle of faith,

we proclaim our faith in God:

who brings us together,

who lights our way,

who comes to us in Jesus.

BENEDICTION OPTIONS

Based on worship theme:

When you are pushed aside and on the edge, may you know God as your constant center, your deepest identity, your true home. In the knowledge of God's eternal love, may you walk this Advent road in faith.

From "Rahab's Blessing" (December 6):

When you are pushed to edges,
>   may you insist on your own story with such grit and grace
>   that they have no choice but to tell it.

When you are far from center,
>   may you know the power and freedom
>   that God grants to those on the margins.

When you face impossible choices,
>   may you act with integrity and courage,
>   resting in the shield of God's grace.

When others dismiss you with a label,
>   may you claim your deep identity
>   as a beloved child of the Creator.

Advent 3

RUTH: A JOURNEY OF LOVE

Scripture reading: Ruth 1:1–18

SERMON SUGGESTIONS

Ruth's decision to travel to Bethlehem with Naomi provides an opportunity to explore the choices we face in our own lives. Your sermon might touch on the ways that different factors such as loyalty, longing, emptiness, bravery, and love influence our decisions. This passage is discussed in the reflection for December 7.

CANDLE-LIGHTING LITURGY
Scripture reading: 1 John 4:7–9

Litany:

Leader: Beloved, we gather in love for God and love for each other.

All: ***We gather to experience God's love for us.***

Leader: God's love is revealed in the stories we hear,

All: ***in the songs we sing,***
in the prayers we offer,

Leader: in the Spirit we feel moving within and among us. God's love is revealed most deeply through Jesus,

All: ***whose coming we anticipate and celebrate,***
who was sent by God so that we might have life.

Leader: Beloved, we gather together for worship.

Lighting the third Advent candle (love):
As we light this candle of love,
we celebrate our love for God
and our love for each other.

We receive the abundant love God offers to us
through the coming of Jesus Christ.

BENEDICTION OPTIONS

Based on worship theme:

For whatever journey lies ahead, may God grant you commitment and courage to choose the faithful path. And may God grant you love—love to give and to receive; love over and around and within you; love to guide each holy step.

From "Ruth's Blessing" (December 13):

May you have courage
to leave where you've been,
to travel to where you're going,
and to do what needs to be done when you get there.
May you have indifference
about how much credit you get,
how many times they say thank you,
and whether or not they call you by name.
May you have wisdom
in the work you choose,
the roles you fill,
and the generosity you exhibit.
And through it all—
in and around and under and above it all—
may you be guided by love.

Advent 4

BATHSHEBA: CONSIDERING POWER

Scripture reading: 1 Kings 1:11–18; [19–28]; 29–31

SERMON SUGGESTIONS

This story of Bathsheba advocating for her son is likely unfamiliar for many people in the congregation. While the Bathsheba we meet in 2 Samuel is mostly silent and passive, here we meet a woman who speaks up and takes risks. This story provides an opportunity to talk about who holds power and how we use power. In the context of Advent, we can talk about what the incarnation says about the power of God. For discussions of power in Bathsheba's story, see the reflections for December 15, 17, and 18.

CANDLE-LIGHTING LITURGY

Scripture reading: Luke 1:30–35

Litany:

Leader: We gather in holy space to hear holy words:

    All: Do not be afraid.

Leader: We gather in holy time to hear a holy promise:

    All: Mary's son will reign forever.

Leader: We gather in this holy moment to sense the holy in our midst:

    All: Let the Holy Spirit come upon us.
    Let the power of the Most High overshadow us.

Leader: Let us worship the Holy One with anticipation and joy.

Lighting the fourth Advent candle (power):
As we light this candle of power,
    we contemplate the power of God
    that created the heavens and the earth,
    that has brought down the powerful from their thrones,
    that comes to us in the vulnerable Christ child.

BENEDICTION OPTIONS

Based on worship theme:
For each step you take in this blessed week, may the Holy Spirit be upon you and may the power of the Most High overshadow your life.

From "Bathsheba's Blessing" (December 19):
Receive now this blessing:
    for companions with integrity;
    for moments of delightful abandon;
    for love deep enough to cause grief;
    for consolation.
May you have the power that is your due
    and use that power on behalf of the vulnerable—
    even if the vulnerable one is you.
May you write your own story,
    and may it be told by compassionate voices
    in all generations to come.

Christmas 1

MARY: TREASURING AND PONDERING

Scripture reading: Luke 2:1–20

SERMON SUGGESTIONS

The birth of Jesus—Emmanuel, God-with-us—is at once spectacular and ordinary. Throughout the nativity story, Mary is fully present to the wonder of it all; she treasures and ponders all that she experiences. As the calendar year comes to an end, you can invite people to treasure the ways God has been with them in the current year and to ponder where God's creative presence may bubble up in the year to come. For further thoughts on the scripture, see the reflections for December 23 and 24.

CANDLE-LIGHTING LITURGY

Scripture reading: Isaiah 55:6–9

Litany:

Leader: Together we seek the Holy One.
We call upon our God, who is near.

All: *Near in the Christ child we celebrate.*
Near in the Spirit we receive.
Near in the creation we inhabit.

Leader: Together we proclaim Emmanuel—

All: *God-with-us.*

Leader: Together we live Emmanuel.

All: *Thanks be to God.*

Lighting the Christ candle:
As we light the Christ candle,
    we celebrate the birth of our Savior, Jesus.
Along with Mary we seek to treasure this gift
    and to ponder all that Emmanuel means for us.

BENEDICTION OPTIONS

Based on worship theme:
Go forth to treasure this life that God has given you. Take time to ponder the mysterious blessing of Emmanuel—God-with-us. God with us now. God with us always. Amen.

From "Christmas Blessing from Mary" (December 25):
In all that God calls you to do and to be,
    may you have courage
    to say yes to the mystery.

In times of excitement, grief, joy, and fear,
    may you have loved ones
    to offer companionship and blessing.

In the labor of creation,
    may you be strong,
    may you be flexible,
    may you know joy.

May you, beloved child,
    ponder deeply each divine message you hear,
    whether from angel or shepherd.
May you ponder and treasure
    every gift you receive
    from the holy hand of God.

Christmas 2

MARY AND ANNA: FAITH IN COMMUNITY

Scripture reading: Luke 2:21–38

SERMON SUGGESTIONS

The story of Jesus' presentation at the temple highlights Mary's commitment to the religious observances of her faith community. Anna provides an example of someone who has made religious commitments the basis of her life. This story can help us think about our own connections to a particular congregation and to the church more broadly. For more thoughts on this story, see the reflections for December 26 and January 1.

CANDLE-LIGHTING LITURGY

Scripture reading: Psalm 84:1–4

Litany:

> Leader: Our souls long for the courts of the Holy One.
> *All: Our hearts sing for joy to the living God.*
> Leader: The swallow builds a nest for herself in
> God's presence,
> *All: and we find our home here, with God's people.*
> Leader: Happy are those who live in your house, O God.
> *All: Happy are we who have gathered to sing your praise.*

Lighting the Christ candle:

As we light the Christ candle,
> we acknowledge the holiness of this space and of this time.

We proclaim Christ's presence here:
> around us, among us, within us.

BENEDICTION OPTIONS

Based on worship theme:

Even though you will leave the walls of this building,[4] you remain at home with God wherever you go. May you know joy in God's presence this week, and may we all return again to share that joy with each other.

From "Anna's Blessing" (January 2):

May your worship bring joy.

May your fasting bring clarity.

May your prayers be powerful.

May your praise ease the world's fear.

May your words be true.

May you be named and respected
    in the roles that God has given you.

---

4. Note: For online worship contexts, the opening phrase could be: "Even though you will leave this time set apart for worship . . .".

Epiphany
MARY: FOLLOWING THE LIGHT THROUGH FEAR
Scripture reading: Matthew 2:1–12; (13–18)

SERMON SUGGESTIONS
The story of the magi is familiar to many, but we rarely consider this event from Mary's perspective. Surely she felt joy and wonder at this recognition of her son, but she must have also felt fear at Herod's presence lurking in the background. How do we handle fear in our own lives, and how do we remind ourselves of God's loving power? The reflections for December 27, 28 and January 3 discuss this story.

CANDLE-LIGHTING LITURGY
Scripture reading: Psalm 27: 1, 13–14

Litany for final lighting of Advent and Christ candles:
We light a candle against the fear that skirts around the edges of each day.

(*Light the first Advent candle.*)
We light a candle against the fear the dwells deep within, heavy and hard.

(*Light the second Advent candle.*)
We light a candle for strength.

(*Light the third Advent candle.*)
We light a candle for courage.

(*Light the fourth Advent candle.*)
We light a candle to claim the salvation of God offered to us in Jesus Christ.

(*Light the Christ candle.*)
Emmanuel is our light and our salvation.
Whom shall we fear?

BENEDICTION OPTIONS
Based on worship theme:
Remember that God is your light and your salvation. Be strong. Let your heart take courage. For you live each day in the shelter and protection of divine love.

From "Mary's Blessing" (December 31):
May you know God in your own heart
 and in the heart of your faith community.
May you be brave toward your fear,
 and persistent through deep difficulties.
May you hold your responsibilities faithfully
 and lightly—with grace and joy.
May you teach well
 and learn well.
May you give attention and compassion
 to the lives that surround you,
  and to your own hard and beautiful life.

SMALL GROUP/
SUNDAY SCHOOL GUIDE

Included here is a general outline for small group sessions, and then several suggestions for the content of those sessions. The first set of plans looks at particular themes throughout the devotional, and the last set suggests a schedule for those who wish to focus on particular women. Small groups should adapt the session outline and material to fit their own context.

GENERAL SMALL GROUP SESSION OUTLINE
Opening prayer
Invite group members to share any joys or concerns they would like to offer for prayer. Conclude the sharing with a simple prayer, such as:

> Holy One, Emmanuel,
>
> Thank you for hearing these prayers that we offer for ourselves and for those we love.
>
> Let us be fully present now with each other and with you as we open our hearts to your sacred Word. Amen.

Centering
Spend one to five minutes in a centering activity such as listening to a song, looking at a visual image (maybe one from this book), or simply experiencing silence. It might be helpful to begin and end the time of centering with a chime or bell.

Listening

Read the given text for the session. You might have one or two assigned readers, or go around the group inviting everyone to read a section. Brief passages could be read twice. For longer passages or weeks where multiple passages are suggested, the leader could be prepared to summarize a portion of the text.

Sharing about the text

Discuss the text you have heard. What stands out? What questions do you have? How does this text relate to other parts of Scripture? The devotional reflections can help guide this discussion.

Making connections between text and life

Talk about what God might be saying to you through the text. The "Consider" questions at the end of each devotional can provide guidance for this discussion. The group leader could also suggest the "Connect" activities to the group as a way to engage the material in the week to come.

Closing blessing

You can close the session with the blessing that accompanies the woman you have discussed that week. Alternately, "Sophia's Blessing" (January 6) would be an appropriate conclusion for each session.

THEMATIC PLANS

These plans explore the stories of multiple women around a given theme.

Worship

These sessions align with the material provided in the "Worship Guide."

Week 1. Tamar: Advent Waiting (November 29–30)

Week 2. Rahab: On the Margins (December 2–3)

Week 3. Ruth: A Journey of Love (December 7)

Week 4. Bathsheba: Considering Power (December 15, 17–18)

Week 5. Mary: Treasuring and Pondering (December 23–24)

Week 6. Mary and Anna: Faith in Community (December 26, January 1)

Week 7. Epiphany—Mary: Following the Light through Fear (December 27–28, January 3)

Justice

Week 1. Tamar Refuses Shame (November 30)

Week 2. Rahab on the Edge (December 2–3)

Week 3. Ruth Is Silenced (December 11)

Week 4. Bathsheba Laments (December 15)

Week 5. Bathsheba Approaches Kings (December 17–18)

Week 6. Mary Sings God's Justice (December 22)

Week 7. The Mothers Weep (January 3)

Parenting

Week 1. Women Prepare the Way (November 27)

Week 2. Rahab Survives (December 4)

Week 3: Ruth Gives Birth (December 12)

Week 4: Bathsheba Grieves (December 16)

Week 5: Mary Gives Birth (December 23)

Week 6: Mary Loses Jesus (December 29)

Week 7: The Mothers Weep (January 3)

Gender and sexuality

Some of the readings in this section contain stories of sexualized violence. It is recommended that groups that choose this theme have leaders who understand trauma and that appropriate care is given to those who may experience trauma reactions to the material.

Week 1: Tamar Refuses Shame (November 30)
Week 2: Rahab Acts by Faith (December 5)
Week 3: Ruth Goes to Boaz (December 10)
Week 4: Bathsheba Suffers an Assault (December 14)
Week 5: Bathsheba Approaches King Solomon (December 18)
Week 6: Mary Says Yes (December 20)
Week 7: Sophia Christ Is Present at Creation (January 5)

SPIRITUAL PRACTICES

This theme provides for more of a group experience than a discussion. If using the suggested outline on page 165, replace the "Sharing about the text" and "Making connections between text and life" discussions with the "Connect" activity suggested by the designated devotional.

Week 1. Tamar Grieves (November 28): Offering Our Grief
Materials needed: Stones and cloths or paper towels

In doing this process as a group, keep silence while holding the stones for an extended period (maybe five minutes). Invite sharing around the circle three times, allowing space after each person speaks and giving people the option to pass if they do not want to share. *Round 1:* Simply name the person or people or things you grieve in this season. *Round 2:* Share a bit more about one of the people or things you are grieving. *Round 3:* Share a word, phrase, or thought that brings you comfort in your grief. After the sharing is done, explain that the cloth or paper towel represents God's care and love. Invite people to wrap their grief stone in the cloth.

Suggestion: For the closing, use "Blessing of the Weeping Mothers" (January 4).

Week 2. Rahab Survives (December 4): Drawing Your Prayers
Materials needed: Paper and colored pencils, pens, or markers

Week 3. Ruth Gives Birth (December 12): Visio divina
Materials needed: A copy of *Expecting Emmanuel* for each participant *or* access to the December 12 image from Michelle Burkholder,
which is available for download at bit.ly/Expecting-Emmanuel. People may also want paper and a writing utensil for journaling.

Week 4. Bathsheba Approaches King David (December 17):
Writing Truth to Power
Materials needed: Paper, pens, envelopes, stamps, addresses for people in power; suggestions of relevant issues people might want to
write about

Week 5. Mary Sings God's Justice (December 22): Singing as
Prayer
Materials needed: Device to play music, hymnals, instruments

Rather than just listening to songs as suggested in the devotional,
you can also sing together.

Week 6. Mary Welcomes the Magi (December 27): Gifts of God's
Loving Power
Materials needed: Card stock, scissors, markers, Bibles; other mis-
cellaneous art supplies as desired (patterned paper, glue, glitter, etc.)

Week 7. Mary Escapes to Egypt (December 28): Praying with a
Labyrinth
Materials needed: Access to a walking labyrinth, copies of a finger
labyrinth, or video of a labyrinth walk

PLANS FOCUSED ON BIBLICAL CHARACTERS

Mary

More than seven sessions focus on Mary. The following schedule is suggested:

Week 1. Mary Says Yes (December 20)

Week 2. Mary Visits Elizabeth (December 21–22)

Week 3. Mary Gives Birth (December 23–24)

Week 4. Mary Presents Jesus at the Temple (December 26, January 1)

Week 5. Mary Welcomes the Magi and Escapes to Egypt (December 27–28)

Week 6. Mary Loses Jesus (December 29)

Week 7. Mary Goes to a Party (December 30)

For the characters below, you can cover all the devotionals (not including blessings) that focus on the given character or characters in a seven-week session.

- Tamar and Rahab
- Ruth
- Bathsheba, the Weeping Mothers, and Sophia

RETREAT GUIDE

An Advent retreat provides an opportunity for people to step away from hectic holiday activities and give deep attention to the One whose birth we anticipate. Below is a suggested schedule for a weekend retreat using the material in this book. Content for the worship and small group sessions is provided in the "Worship Guide" and "Small Group/Sunday School Guide" on the previous pages.

FRIDAY EVENING
Share supper together (optional)

Opening Worship: Advent Waiting with Tamar (see Advent 1 worship, p. 150)

For the retreat worship sessions, you do not need a full-length worship service with a sermon. Choose some of the provided liturgy pieces (see p. 151) and a worship song or two. You can use the candle-lighting liturgy *from the Sunday that corresponds to the week of Advent in which the retreat is held.*

Small Group Session #1: On the Margins with Rahab (December 2 and 3)

For guidance in structuring these sessions, see "General Small Group Session Outline" on page 165. If there are fewer than eight retreat participants, everyone can remain together for the small group sessions. Larger retreat groups can be divided into smaller groups for these sessions as seems appropriate for the context.

SATURDAY
Breakfast

Group Spiritual Practice #1: Offering Our Grief (November 28; see instructions on p. 168)

Small Group Session #2: Surviving with Rahab (December 4)

Personal time

Lunch

Small Group Session #3: Journeying with Ruth (December 7)

Personal time

Group Spiritual Practice #2: *Visio divina* (see December 12)

Supper

Small Group Session #4: Considering Power with Bathsheba (December 15, 17, and 18)

Personal/social time

SUNDAY
Breakfast

Small Group Session #5: Saying Yes with Mary (December 20)

Closing Worship: Pondering with Mary (see Christmas 1 worship, p. 159)

End with lunch (optional)

The sessions suggested above journey through Advent with the five women listed in Jesus' genealogy, just touching on Christmas in the closing worship. For a more thematic focus, or to concentrate on fewer characters during the retreat, you can easily adapt the above schedule using any of the small group plans (pp. 165–170):

- For opening worship, use material from devotionals for week 1.
- For small group sessions 1–5, use devotionals for weeks 2–6.
- For closing worship, use material from devotionals for week 7.
- For the two group spiritual practice sessions, choose two of the spiritual practice sessions on pages 168–169.

THE AUTHOR

Joanna Harader serves as pastor of Peace Mennonite Church in Lawrence, Kansas. Her worship liturgies have been published in the *Voices Together* hymnal and are used in churches of various denominations. She has written for publications such as *Christian Century*, *Leader* magazine, and Shine Sunday school curriculum. She writes regularly for the *RevGal Blog Pals* blog, as well as her own blog, *Spacious Faith*.

THE ILLUSTRATOR

Michelle Burkholder serves as the associate pastor of Hyattsville (Maryland) Mennonite Church and is a practicing visual artist. One of Michelle's paper cutout pieces, *Loaves and Fishes*, can be found in the *Voices Together* hymnal. After studying art and theater at Eastern Mennonite University, Michelle went on to study the intersections of theology and the arts at United Theological Seminary of the Twin Cities. The connections between art, faith, and spirituality fill Michelle with wonder, curiosity, and joy.